LOVE AS A GUIDE TO MORALS

VIBS

Volume 249

Robert Ginsberg
Founding Editor

Leonidas Donskis
Executive Editor

Associate Editors

a volume in
Ethical Theory and Practice
ETP
Olli Loukola, Editor

LOVE AS A GUIDE TO MORALS

Andrew Fitz-Gibbon

With a Guest Foreword by
Barry L. Gan

Amsterdam - New York, NY 2012

Cover photo: www.dreamstime.com

Cover Design: Studio Pollmann

The paper on which this book is printed meets the requirements of "ISO 9706:1994, Information and documentation - Paper for documents - Requirements for permanence".

ISBN: 978-90-420-3530-0
E-Book ISBN: 978-94-012-0805-5
© Editions Rodopi B.V., Amsterdam - New York, NY 2012
Printed in the Netherlands

Ethical Theory and Practice (ETP)

Olli Loukola
Editor

Other Titles in ETP

Michael H. Mitias. *Friendship: A Central Moral Value.* 2012. VIBS 239

True love in every moment praises God.
Longing love brings a sorrow sweet to the pure.
Seeking love belongs to itself alone.
Understanding love gives itself equally to all.
Enlightened love is mingled with the sadness of the world.
But selfless love bears an effortless fruit,
working so quietly even the body cannot say
how it comes and goes.

Mechtild of Magdeburg

Love's hidden life is in the innermost being, unfathomable,
and then in turn is in an unfathomable connectedness with all existence.

Søren Kierkegaard

For Larry Ashley,
Mentor,
Good Friend,
Squash Player, and
Philosopher's Philosopher

CONTENTS

EDITORIAL FOREWORD

Ethical questions are the primary questions of human existence. No matter what else we do in our lives, sooner or later, ethical issues arise seriously affecting our relationships, choices, and actions. At the same time, the language of ethics contains an illusion of straightforwardness and immediate understanding. Just as is the case with ordinary language, most of us are fully competent to use it, capable of expressing ourselves through it, and getting things done with it, sometimes debating, other time agreeing. Ethics are integral to who we are.

The paradigmatic mode for ethical language and discussion was set by Socrates with his dialectical method some two and a half thousand years ago. The Socratic dialogues contain the same deceptive illusion of easiness, straightforwardness, and simplicity. They are comfortably readable and understandable with no prior philosophical expertise, and surely—as historians have shown—Plato wrote them with this goal in mind. Yet this apparent simplicity never diminished their value as philosophical texts in any manner, and as we all know, the dialogues were, in fact, the starting point of the philosophical enquiry of morality of our civilization.

This appearance of straightforwardness of ethical issues sometimes cloaks the fact that answers to ethical dilemmas are hardly ever easy to find. Moreover, it gives layperson no indication of the fact that philosophical ethical inquiry is a highly specialized, technical, and abstract skill, a *techné*. Thus, the illusion of easiness of ethical discussion is deceptive indeed. Ethical enquiry begins from the various human projections, reflections, and viewpoints concerning ethical life. In this examination, it utilizes a variety of techniques, empirical and theoretical data, conceptual analysis and argumentation, and a range of methods and frames of reference. It is just this sort of ethical inquiry is the explicit goal of this special series, Ethical Theory and Practice (ETP), where this book is now published; that is, to describe, examine, and analyze ethical issues through the understanding afforded to us by the various academic disciplines. It is an enormously rich field of inquiry, bordering at the far extremes of theory and practice.

The volume at hand, *Love as a Guide to Morals*, represents the goal of ETP par excellence. At face value, it is highly readable, enticing, and fascinating, following the best traditions of philosophical writing; yet at the same time, it contains careful argumentation, detailed analysis, and enlightening insights in the very same vein as the best of ethical inquiries. Text such as this one would simply not be possible without thorough familiarity of ethical issues, their philosophical underpinnings, and the methods used in their study. Thus, the illusion of easiness of ethical discussion still prevails, but here, as in best philosophical dialogues, the discussion is interwoven within the rich and multifaceted fabric of our history, philosophy, and civilization. The easiness is not an empty illusion here; quite the contrary, it is straightforwardness created by roots common to all human beings, familiarity of the topics discussed, understanding of the issues involved, and most importantly, by the recognition of their importance to us all.

Olli Loukola, Editor
Ethical Theory and Practice

Guest Foreword

Plato's dialogues do not mark the beginning of Western philosophy, nor do they mark its culmination. But in many respects, they mark its high point, ancient though they are. They are works of art, works of logic, works of literature, ethics, law, and more. Because the quality of Plato's dialogues is so high, they have come to epitomize that literary form and are, arguably, the most engaging philosophical writings of all time. Andrew Fitz-Gibbon's *Love as a Guide to Morals* is also a dialogue, very much in the mold and spirit of Plato's dialogues. As such, his book is in the finest tradition of philosophy, East or West.

Since I first met Andy Fitz-Gibbon some years ago, we have had many discussions on love and nonviolence. Our discussions have themselves been very similar to those among the characters in this dialogue, but the main antagonist in the dialogue, though he bears my name, is not I. Because this book focuses on many of the themes that Andy and I have touched upon throughout the years, I am very pleased to provide this foreword.

Though our talks over the years have centered more on nonviolence than on love, our discussions often circled around to discussions about love and ethics, too. As Andy says, "love-itself is always nonviolent." Naturally.

Four features of the dialogue stand out. First, of course, is the dialogue's exploration of love and its relation to ethics. Second is the form itself, the dialogue. Third is the dialogue's tone, which reflects very well many aspects of the content. And fourth is the sheer breadth of the dialogue.

Plato and Empedocles were the first Western philosophers to speak about love. Fitz-Gibbon speaks explicitly of Plato's *Symposium* but does not mention Empedocles. While this may be deliberate, insofar as Empedocles' notion of love is applicable to all of nature and thus, more universal than is Fitz-Gibbon's, it is also true that Fitz-Gibbon's account of love could play off that of Empedocles. Empedocles contrasts love with strife, much as Fitz-Gibbon implicitly does. Thus, the virtues that, according to Fitz-Gibbon, love comprises, virtues such as kindness, gentleness, non-harm, faithfulness, and others, clearly run counter to the idea of strife.

Interestingly, too, though Fitz-Gibbon is concerned with human behavior as choice and not laws of nature as such, he is also speaking clearly of a much broader notion of love than is suggested by usage of the term in contemporary culture or even in Plato. In this, this work also resembles Empedocles, though Fitz-Gibbon's concept of love is not as broad, limited pointedly as it is to the realm of human choice.

Just as Martin Luther King Jr. sought to expand awareness of the concept of love from that of romantic passion, *eros*, to include fondness or friendship, *philia*, and especially respect of others, *agape*, Fitz-Gibbon adds another: affection, which he places in terms of intensity and intimacy after *eros* and *philia* and before *agape*.

However, this dialogue is not a mere exercise in analyzing the concept of love. It realizes the heart of its content through its form and tone. In the penultimate act of his dialogue, Fitz-Gibbon identifies twelve virtues of love. These virtues must be practiced daily as actions, he says, to acquire the virtue as part of one's character. The dialogue itself exemplifies both the action and the character: the characters in this dialogue are always amiable, gentle, kind, and, in short, loving. The same can be said for the overall tone of the dialogue. In fact, the very title of the book, *Love as a Guide to Morals,* reflects the broader content in several ways: in the first place, the book speaks of itself as a guide, not a rulebook; as a guide, not an instruction manual. The very word "guide" itself suggests a loving attitude, that of a friend. In that spirit, Fitz-Gibbon strives to illustrate, throughout the dialogue, that friendship is, indeed, a kind of love, very much in the way that a parent might love a child or that one friend might care for another—as a guide or companion.

By refusing to treat love as a rule, in contrast to Joseph Fletcher, whose *Situation Ethics* is discussed within, Fitz-Gibbon does more than bow toward feminist ethics. He mirrors many feminist approaches to ethics and implicitly if not explicitly rejects masculine approaches, which are rule-based and focused on duties or rights.

Any dialogue, by its very nature, involves the reader as participant far more than mere essays do. Fitz-Gibbon, deliberately, one might infer, includes in the dialogue two men and two women, and though one woman is a student, the respect she is accorded, the amiability with which she is included, says much about how Fitz-Gibbon understands *philia* and *affection.* The fourth character is also female, a colleague and peer, and the protagonist relies on her expertise for constructive suggestions when she enters the dialogue.

Although Fitzgibbon's focus is on love as a guide to morals, it also serves, quite deliberately, I think, to provide those new to philosophy with a rather comprehensive portrait of the field. One is introduced to questions of God, metaphysics, epistemology, aesthetics, logic, and, of course ethics, among others. Moreover, the discussion is by no means limited to Western philosophy. Buddhism, Chinese philosophy, and the thought of Gandhi are also to be found within. Ethics is discussed in somewhat more detail, to be sure. And so, while this volume may be viewed as a treatise on love with respect to morality, it also serves well as an introductory text in philosophy.

Many of the philosophical questions introduced in this text can be pursued in greater depth by attention to the dialogue's footnotes, which provide reference to quite a few of the great works of philosophy, past and present, East and West. Were one to read the works recommended in the footnotes themselves, one would have completed at least the equivalent of an undergraduate if not a master's degree, in philosophy. They offer the book's readers excellent background and sources with which they can pursue more deeply the many philosophical topics raised and discussed in the dialogue. Thus, the volume serves several pedagogical uses.

My discussions with Andy Fitz-Gibbon over the years have led me to broaden my understanding of love, and my friendship with him has led me to admire just how well he incorporates his intellectual work with his daily life. Finally, this volume makes clarifies his Aristotelian approach to life: the cultivation of daily habits that lead one to develop a virtuous character. In Fitz-Gibbon's particular case, these daily habits are the twelve virtues he identifies as constitutive of a loving life, and his book is something of a primer on how to cultivate just such a life.

Barry L. Gan
Professor of Philosophy
St. Bonaventure University

PREFACE

Adam, Barry and Molly (and a few minor characters) exist only in the pages of this book. Nonetheless, the idea that gave rise to them occurred on the squash courts at the State University of New York, College at Cortland. Here, two real-life philosophers, Larry Ashley and I, have enjoyed the delightful game of squash and our equally animated discussions. One day, we joked that we ought to write up our "squash court conversations." I had been intending to write on love and morality for some time, and when I set my thoughts down in writing, they came out in conversational form.

Philosophy written as conversation is an important method that began with the greatest of all philosophers, Plato, in his Socratic dialogues. Much philosophy, even when not in an overtly conversational form, is written with imaginary critics in mind, whom the author answers in often-convoluted ways. To write intentionally in a realistic conversation form may avoid some of the complexities involved in writing against imaginary critics. It also means writing in as jargon-free language as possible. Even so, a fly on the squash court wall would have heard many more "ums," "errs," half sentences, and grunts than I have included in the conversation here! In reality, our thoughts are often expressed with less coherence than Adam and Barry display in the pages of this book.

Of necessity, I have omitted from the conversation quotations by other philosophers and relevant works, but pertinent ones can be found in the endnotes following each of the six acts.

In the conversation, Adam speaks more or less in my voice, while Barry raises the kind of objections, questions, and comments that my good friend and mentor Larry does. Yet, Barry is not Larry and I am not suggesting that the remarks Barry makes are those of Larry Ashley. Nonetheless, I am deeply grateful for our ongoing and extended discussions about the subject of this book and numerous other subjects.

Molly is a more fictive character, though I daresay some of my women friends and colleagues, at the State University of New York College at Cortland and beyond, may hear echoes of themselves in her voice.

This book had its genesis in a paper I read at the 2005 annual conference of the North American Society for Social Philosophy. The ideas were, at that time, undeveloped, and more of a seed than an established plant. Nonetheless, I was grateful for the very kind and constructive critique I received, and for comments on a subsequent paper I submitted for publication. Over the next several years I developed the ideas testing out notions of love and nonviolence, the ethics of care, love and morality, and loving praxis.

The title pays homage to Iris Murdoch's remarkable *Metaphysics as a Guide to Morals*, which summarizes her eminent career as a philosopher and writer.[1]

Conversations are too many to recount, but I am grateful for significant moments along the way, with thanks to R. Paul Churchill, David Boersema, Danielle Poe, Joseph Betz, Helen Codd, Michael Smith, many colleagues at the State University of New York, College at Cortland, especially Kathy Russell, Mecke Nagel, Joseph Rayle, Judith Ouillette and Amy Henderson-Harr, students in all my classes, especially the Ethics of Love, and participants in the sundry conferences where I have given papers tangential to the themes in this book. Marked thanks to Olli Loukola, VIBS Ethical Theory and Practice Series Editor (and some time squash player) for including the book in his series. Eric Van Broekhuizen, VIBS Executive Editor, gave helpful encouragement and advice. Barry Gan has written a very kind guest foreword, for which I thank him. Elizabeth D. Boepple, copy-editor extraordinaire, as ever, nicely polished my writing. My wife Jane has lived the subject of this book with me for thirty-six years. We have learned together how to love—*amo: volo ut sis.*

Most of the ideas in the book I thrashed out with my very good friend Larry Ashley on, and off, the squash court. If I am a better philosopher than I was, it is in large part because of Larry, and it is to him I dedicate the book.

Andrew Fitz-Gibbon, Associate Professor, and Chair
Department of Philosophy
Director of the Center for Ethics, Peace, and Social Justice
State University of New York College at Cortland

Act I

LOVE AND MORALITY

Scene 1

Wednesday, late afternoon, sometime in January, on the way to the university squash courts. Colleagues and friends, Barry and Adam walk briskly in the winter cold. Salted snow turned to slush clings to their winter boots. Barry is an American analytical philosopher, atheist, and materialist. Adam is a British expatriate, ethicist, theist, and idealist.

Barry: You look pleased with yourself. Anything special?

Adam: No, not really. I have just been thinking how much I love my job.

Barry: Ah, you've had a good class then?

Adam: Yes, my senior seminar on philosophies of nonviolence. I really enjoy it when students finally grasp an important idea. It makes teaching worthwhile. It never ceases to amaze me how inquisitive we human beings are.

Barry: [*pulling up the collar of his battered L.L. Bean olive green winter coat*] We're like most animals, really, but we articulate our questions in a way non-human animals can't. That's what led me to philosophy as a discipline. I've always been fascinated by the large questions. Among my favorite are, "Why is there something rather than nothing and what is that something?" and "How do we know what we think we know?"

Adam: These are all great questions! They've exercised the minds of philosophers for centuries.[1]

Barry: That other conundrum, "What is beautiful and what makes it so?" is a close third for me.[2]

Adam: [*giving a short laugh*] Another tricky one! But as you know, my pressing interest lies elsewhere. The question "How should we live?" really grips me. It's the basic ethical problem and reaches into every area of human life.[3] Actually, I have been working through a few ideas for a new book that I'd like to discuss with you.

Barry: Wonderful! What's it about?

Adam: It's about love and morality.

Barry: Sounds interesting. Have you thought of a title?

Adam: I have a provisional one: *Love as a Guide to Morals*. I have a good idea of where I'm going with the book, but some of my thoughts need sharpening. I was hoping you could help me.

Barry: That's fine by me. I always enjoy our squash-court chats. What's on your mind?

Adam: I want my book to be well reasoned, yet practical. I'm trying to steer a clear course between a book that's philosophically worthwhile, and one that's accessible to non-philosophers.

Barry: [*smiling*] Ah, "caught between Scylla and Charybdis."[4] That's always difficult. A great deal of philosophy seems to be irredeemably complex. But, when it's over-simplified it may not stand up to scrutiny.

Adam: Exactly! You and I have agreed before that far too much philosophical discussion excludes ordinary folk. It can be very elitist. To be of use, philosophy needs to be a public discourse—one available to any average, reasonably educated person.

Barry: Yes, I agree. But you still need to make a good argument. It should be one that's both logically valid—its conclusion should follow from its premises—and it should be sound. The premises of the argument must be true. You wouldn't want to lose something in translation between the academy and the marketplace . . . [*grinning*] Perhaps now we should say between the academy and the shopping mall. So, what are you thinking?[5]

Adam: Although the great philosophical questions are perennial, at different times, one area is more in vogue than others. Take, for example, the question of existence. In differing ways, it gripped the minds of medieval philosophers, modern scientists, and twentieth-century existentialists alike. Another example is René Descartes, the first truly modern philosopher, who began a trend in the theory of knowledge with his famous "*cogito ergo sum*,"[6] "I think, therefore I am." He sparked a whole new trend in thinking about knowledge.

Barry: I'm getting the picture. So you might say that during the nineteenth century, the Romantics looked intensely into beauty. It became very fashionable and exercised the minds of philosophers for a while. Then the trend changed.

Adam: That's it! Presently, there is a discernable turn toward ethical questions.[7]

Barry: I agree and that's not surprising. Questions arise in response to cultural events, as people try to make sense of their present existence. Some of the greatest and most enduring works of philosophy were written in response to some change in society. In part, Plato's *Republic* was a response to the Peloponnesian War between Athens and Sparta. Augustine's *City of God* found its context in the imminent collapse of the Roman Empire. *The Communist Manifesto* was written in a few short weeks amid the earth-shaking changes of the industrial revolution in Britain and mid-nineteenth-century European social revolutions.[8]

Adam: It would seem reasonable, then, that the tumultuous twentieth century would bring in its wake an urgent return to the question of how we should live. The century gave us the most enormous advances in technology in human history. Yet, it was also the bloodiest and most destructive. Ethics tries to make sense of that.

Barry: I assume, then, that you are meaning ethics in its broadest sense.

Adam: [*frowning slightly*] Yes, it worries me that morality has become something we think of as purely private, usually involving sex or money. Philosophical ethics is much broader than that. Whenever we talk about "ought to" or "should" we are using moral language. Though, I do prefer "should" language to "ought" as "ought" implies some kind of sanction if the ought is not fulfilled.[9] It becomes too legalistic for me. Still, as Immanuel Kant taught us, ought language is ethical language. But, it's bad philosophy to make morality private and everything else social, political, or business, as if we no longer ought to engage in the necessary task of thinking ethically about all of life. How we live includes every kind of social interaction and more.

Barry: You would include politics, family life, work life, religion, and relationships between nations.

Adam: Even further! It includes our relationship with non-human animals, with all of sentient life, and the whole of our environment.

Barry: [*smiling*] That's a huge subject—and you feel you have something to say about the whole? I can't wait, but it will be a tall order and it will have to be a good argument to satisfy me.

Scene 2

Barry and Adam arrive at the locker room and begin to prepare for their much-awaited game of squash. They chat as they get ready for the games to come. Adam returns to the discussion . . .

Adam: So, let me try to get to the heart of what I want to write about. One answer to how we should live—in recent history proposed most popularly by Mahatma Gandhi in India and most eloquently by Martin Luther King Jr. in the United States—is that we should live a life of love.[10]

Barry: [*fiddling with the wrapping on his racquet handle*] I must get a new one of these. It hardly stays on anymore. Sorry Adam! Hmm, I deeply respect both Gandhi and King, but haven't many looked at their ideas and rejected them? This world pragmatism would say that love is fine for children and lovers, but impractical as a guide to morals for adults. We need something less romantic and more realistic, don't you think? Love is simply not an adequate basis for morality.

Adam: [*excitedly*] I want to make an argument for just the opposite. Your skepticism means you will be a fine conversation partner as I develop my ideas. My view is that moral philosophers have not taken love seriously enough—though this is beginning to change.

Barry: So more philosophers are looking at the concept of love now?

Adam: Yes. In 1970, Iris Murdoch said, "We need a moral philosophy in which the concept of love, so rarely mentioned now by philosophers, can once again be made central."[11] Since then, a number of philosophers have taken up the challenge.

Barry: Any I might know?

Adam: I'll mention two of the most significant. Irving Singer wrote an impressive trilogy that covered the philosophical and literary treatment of love from Plato to the modern world.[12] Alan Soble, too, has a number of impressive works on the philosophy of love.[13] I should also say that there are scientific and social science accounts of love that add to our understanding,[14] not to mention the many religious works that give an account of love. However, these impressive philosophical works on love do not specifically address Murdoch's request for a *moral* philosophy of love.[15] In my book, I want to begin to fill the gap by making a philosophical argument that love is a helpful guide to morals.

The two philosophers concentrate on their squash gear for a few minutes. Barry finishes fastening his knee braces and turns to Adam.

Barry: Okay. Let me hear your argument on the way to the court. I think we're in number five today.

Adam: To put my thesis simply, love has a unifying power for morality and is more suited to ethical thinking and practice than any other idea. The world would tend toward greater flourishing and have far less suffering if people were more loving.

Barry: [*scratching his beard*] I doubt anyone would disagree, but for me, it sounds too simplistic. I guess I'll see as your argument develops.

Adam: My thesis will be a type of Aristotelian argument that sees love as the telos of life. The habits of love produce the virtues of a loving life.

Barry: Of the ancient Western philosophers, I have soft spot for Aristotle. But I do have some issues with his ideas. It will be interesting to see if you address them. [*pausing in thought*] Before we go any further, I need to ask why you chose love over other values. It sounds to me as if you have already reached your conclusion before providing an argument why it must be so. [*playfully raising an eyebrow*] Love is my answer; now let me find an argument to support it.

Adam: [*mildly laughing*] Of course, that's a danger. Yet, what you accuse me of is always true to some degree. None of us begins an enquiry with a blank slate. The most hard-nosed, data-driven science begins with a hypothesis. There are assumptions, presuppositions, and prejudgments already in place. Community, socialization, education, and experience shape these. They are better acknowledged than assumed not to exist.[16]

Barry: [*frowning slightly, showing impatience*] Of course, I agree. But, why privilege love in the way you do?

Adam: Earlier in our conversation, you said that my argument must be valid and sound.

Barry: I recall.

Adam: I agreed, but I will also add to those criteria the idea of coherence. By that I mean that belief about anything is justified by its being a member of a coherent set of beliefs.[17] So, my starting place is a long tradition in which love has been proposed as a reasonable guide to morals. In other words, my thesis is not novel. It has historical roots in ancient Daoism and Confucian benevolence, in Hindu *ahimsa,* in Buddhist loving kindness, in Jewish wisdom, Christian love, and Islamic compassion. I think I can also make a good case for Kant's categorical imperative as a form of love. Adam Smith's "fellow-feeling" and David Hume's sympathy are all ways of speaking about love. And, of course, feminist philosophers have turned their attention to caring as a basis for ethics. In fact, I will suggest that care is one of the virtues of the practice of love. So you can see that there has been a long and coherent tradition of philosophical and theological thinking about love in human experience. I want to take another look at this tradition, test its validity, and add my own modifications. In the process, I hope to provide an argument for why love is a good guide to morals.

Barry: Some of those traditions about love seem obvious, others less so.

Adam: If I can give you an analogy: A structure is already in place. The task is to build a better house. It is not that we are starting from scratch. We might want to rebuild plank-by-plank, even add an extension; perhaps tear down a few old things. The finished product may be radically different from the one we start with.[18] Yet, we do start somewhere.

Barry: [*smiling*] I'll concede the point [*pausing*] for now. Using your analogy, what new structures will you add? I'm thinking of something about love that has not been said before.

Adam: In the philosophy of love, there have been two broad traditions: "erosic" love and "agapic" love. Philosophers have most commonly said that while agapic love (meaning altruistic, disinterested love, such as compassion) may be a good guide to morals, erosic love (sexual love, particularistic love) is not. I will suggest that love, in all its complexity, is a guide to morals. I will take a holistic view of love rather than dualistic.

Barry: [*gently pulling his beard*] Hmm. So you will establish that there is a long tradition of thinking about love, but what is the connection of love to morality?

Adam: I will suggest that love in practice looks very much like what I call the four prima facie principles of morality: nonmaleficence (or no-harm), respect for loved-ones and their community, justice for loved one when they face injustice, and beneficence (or seeking good for the loved-one).[19]

Barry: I have used similar ideas with my students. I assume you will explore the complexity of these principles.

Adam: Yes.

Barry: That these principles are as close to universals that we can find, in that all the great philosophical and religious traditions have them in some form or another.

Adam: Yes.

Barry: That some are more clearly universal than others; no-harm and respect, for instance.

Adam: Yes.

Barry: That there is tension between respecting the autonomy of the individual and community responsibilities and values.

Adam: Yes.

Barry: That when you say justice you are not thinking merely of criminal justice, but issues like equality and fairness.

Adam: Yes.

Barry: That it is not as obvious that you ought to work for the good of the Other as is that you ought not to harm the Other.

Adam: Yes.

Barry: [*grinning broadly*] I've trained you well!

Adam: [*smiling back*] You have!

Barry: But, what's the connection of these four principles to love?

Adam: My claim is that these four prima facie principles of morality are all ways of speaking about loving concern. When I truly love the Other, then my loving concern will be worked out in those four foundational moral ways. Lovers seek always the good of the Other. They seek never to harm the Other. They respect the personhood and integrity of the Other. They seek justice for the Other. It is this multi-faceted loving concern that makes love a suitable guide for morals.

Barry: Well, it sounds like the beginning of an interesting argument. [*frowning*] So, you reduce all morality to love, then?

Adam: I don't like your idea of reduction. But yes, all morality is a function of loving relationships.

Barry: I wait to be convinced!

Adam: I don't expect that all my readers will agree with me about love and morality. That would be folly.

Barry: Folly indeed!

Adam: But, I do hope that readers will come some way with me, adjust and refine their views. I hope that their ethical viewpoint will be affected by love. [*pausing*] We've talked for so long that we've nearly used all our time. Come on, let's play squash.

Adam begins to walk toward the locker room door.

Barry: [*picking up Adam's squash racquet*] But don't forget this. We wouldn't have much of a game!

Adam: [*laughing*] It's your fault! You've got me so engaged in my project! Thanks! [*taking his racquet*]

They leave the locker room.

Scene 3

Squash Court 5. Adam and Barry have played a few games. They are leaning on opposite walls. Both are a little breathless.

Barry: Are you saying that love is the only basis for morality? To put it another way, that we have no ethical theory available that is not based on love? Can you be more specific?

Adam: Let me expand a little. Let's think about boiling water for a cup of tea. There are a number of different ways to boil water.

Barry: OK, I'll play along. There is a range top with water in a kettle or pan. There is an electric kettle. There is a microwave oven. Will that do?

Adam: Yes. Each of those ways is possible. You wouldn't say that an electric kettle is the only way to heat the water. In a similar way, I am not saying that love is the *only* basis for morality. Love is but one among many possibilities. Other contenders for a basis of the moral life have included a set of rules to be followed, maximizing pleasure and minimizing pain, and basing morality in rights or in contract. Philosophers make good arguments for each, and each is a sufficient basis for moral reasoning. However, my idea is that love is not only one amongst a number of sufficient bases for morality, but that love is a better basis than all the others.

Barry: [*smiling wryly*] In a way, you could argue that the electric kettle is the best among a number of sufficient bases for heating water.

Adam: So, I will argue that love is the best among a number of ways of thinking morally. But, I will venture a little further. All the bases for the moral life, at their best, approximate to love.

Barry: [*furrowing eyebrows*] Your argument will need to be carefully reasoned! Love is such a complex idea—as slippery as a wet fish! It's more multifarious than simply boiling water.

Adam: [*laughing while re-tying the laces on his squash shoes*] I realize that, and I'm not claiming that my account of love is the only one. It is the nature and the beauty of love that there are many different tellings. Prose, poetry, theater, and cinema may be better media to convey thoughts about love than reasoned argument. A picture painted in a fleeting moment by a great actor on stage may speak more than a treatise of words. Love is in the look, the feeling, and the gesture. [*in a bad British-French accent*] *Le cœur a ses raisons que la raison ne connaît point.*[20]

Barry: Blaise Pascal's old dictum! "The heart has its reasons, which reason does not know." So now, we give up reason altogether.

Adam: [*mildly irritated*] You know me better than that! Of course, we have to think, and our thinking is better for being logical. Yet, I don't want to sacrifice love's enigmatic indefinability. Ethics, like aesthetics, is more than logic and more than rationality alone. Philosophers such as John MacMurray, Robert Solomon, and Martha Nussbaum have made strong arguments for including emotion alongside reasoning as a major part of the ethical process. I will make an argument that it is the suprarational, transcategorical nature of love that makes it particularly suited to guide the way we live. It is not neat and tidy, but then, neither is life.[21]

Barry: Good. You say that love is a sufficient basis for morality (and perhaps the best basis), but [*emphasizing by pointing his finger*] is love necessary for morality? Going back to your heating water for tea, though there may be any number of sufficient ways to heat the water, some things are necessary. For example, a source of heat is necessary. So, is love necessary?

Adam: Ultimately, I will say yes, to live a moral life requires love. You will need to see how my argument about love develops to show this. But, in a popular understanding, you can live a type of moral life and not be a very loving person! I know plenty of unloving people whose lives would be described as quite moral, at least in a formal sense. They do "the right thing," yet with none of the warmth of love. Some types of morality can be quite harsh.

Barry: But, even provisionally, you will allow that *some* things are necessary for any kind of morality to be possible?

Adam: Of course! Some basic ideas must be true for us to have any discussion about ethics. If any of these are not true, then the enterprise falls at the first hurdle. I take for granted, first, that morality is a worthwhile enterprise and moral language is meaningful.[22]

Barry: [*laughing*] Quite an assumption!

Adam: Second, I assume that people have an innate sympathy for other human beings and, at least, for some other sentient beings.

Barry: Ah! This sounds like David Hume.[23] His argument was that reason is a slave to the passions. Though most philosophers have suggested that reason ought to guide—even control—the emotions, Hume thought that emotions guide reason.

Adam: Yes, I will include Hume and his theory of sentiment. His friend Adam Smith also said something very similar about "fellow feeling." For them, it is innate sympathy that forms the basis of morality.[24] They hold that human beings are "hard-wired" with sympathy for other human beings. It is this sympathy that is the beginning of our moral sense and our moral actions.

Barry: But, you will allow that sociopaths don't share this innate sympathy?

Adam: Yes, I allow that. It may well be that the sociopath has no moral sense, but we can't base our general ideas on such exceptions.

Barry: I suppose so.

Adam: [*smiling*] And you are right about my Humean leanings here. How deep human sympathy is, what the content of it may be, whether it's biologically or socially constructed in the early years of life, matters not. The fact of sympathy—that we are interested in the lives of others—is necessary for the moral task. [*pausing in thought*] I also assume that human beings have the capacity to choose. Their lives are not completely determined, biologically, socially, by fate, or by divine fiat.[25]

Barry: [*tugging at his beard*] Let me summarize. You say that necessary for any kind of morality are: first, that moral language is meaningful, then, that human beings have an innate sympathy, and finally that people have the ability to make choices, that all is not determined. I think you have said it well, though on another occasion, I would want a discussion about each of those "metaethical issues," as we call them. Perhaps, on another day!

Adam: I think so. I won't have space enough in my book to make an argument for these necessary conditions, but I'd take it as a starting place that they are true.

Barry: [*taking off his glasses and rubbing his eyes*] I have so many questions rumbling round my over-used brain! Let me try a few more before we play another game. How would you situate your understanding of love as a guide to morals vis-à-vis the classical philosophical understandings of deontology, consequentialism, and virtue?[26]

Adam: Those who write about love and morality haven't been in agreement. Some have suggested that love is thoroughly deontological—about motivation, about duty. You love your neighbor purely out of duty, without consideration of the consequences to yourself or even to your neighbor.

Barry: While duty makes some moral sense, I've always found the argument that consequences don't matter hard to swallow! Common sense tells us outcomes matter.

Adam: I agree. And we both differ from Kant, who argued that an act is moral insofar as it is a fulfillment of duty regardless of the consequences.[27] He said that because we don't have control over consequences, but we do have control over our own choices, motivations, and intentions. For Kant, morality is all about the exercise of a good will. It's an interesting point. Yet, it's not the whole story. Clearly, consequences matter and have a direct effect on any duties we may have. In that light, some have suggested that love, as a guide to morals, should have a consequentialist basis. You act in such a way as to produce the most loving consequences. Joseph Fletcher made a strong argument for this in the mid-1960s as a kind of utilitarianism.

Barry: In utilitarianism, if you want to act morally, you'll make your best guess at the possible consequences of your actions, and then take the action that will maximize the utility. The utility is usually pleasure. So, the action that will maximize pleasure and minimize pain will always be the right action to take. For Fletcher, would love be the utility to be maximized?

Adam: Yes. I've always appreciated the way that utilitarians make the distinction between the "good" and the "right." The good is that which we desire the most. When you have determined the good, the right is always to maximize the good. Fletcher simply changed pleasurable outcomes for loving outcomes. For him, love is the summum bonum—Latin for the highest good—the good to be maximized.

Barry: Wouldn't his argument depend on what he meant by love.

Adam: Yes. For Fletcher, love is the same as a benevolent outcome, the neighbor's good.[28] For a utilitarian, the neighbor includes all affected by the consequences of an action. So, loving outcomes are good outcomes.

Barry: True utilitarians will also say that no action in and of itself is a moral action. Because morality is dependent on consequences, morality is always situational.

Adam: Fletcher fits the bill! He argues that loving actions will differ given different circumstances, so that the same action may be considered moral in one situation and immoral in another. He is a thoroughgoing situationist. In this way, he could argue that the dropping of the atomic bomb on Hiroshima, in August 1945, was the most loving thing to do. He made a utility calculation that concluded that by dropping the bomb more people would know well-being than by not dropping the bomb. The consequences of not dropping the bomb would have been many more deaths in continued conventional warfare, and, hence less loving.[29]

Barry: Nuclear warfare as an act of love!

Adam: So he argued. For Fletcher, love is a calculation (more so than others in the love and morality tradition). I find some of his ideas difficult.

Barry: I would agree. There is something not quite right about "calculating love." Surely, love is more a feeling and is not reducible to mere rational calculation?

Adam: Yes, love is a feeling. But, I wouldn't go so far as to say that rationality is excluded. There is a long tradition that suggests that love is more than mere feeling. It is the tradition that says, "Love your enemies. Love your neighbor as yourself." For love to be commanded requires at least some thought and the ability to choose.

Barry: I am glad you raised this issue. For me, this gets to the heart of the problem of love and morality. There is an "oughtness" about morality. Kant called it the "imperative"—a kind of obligation. I have always found it strange that love can be commanded. You can't tell someone to "fall in love." To be in love is more like something that happens to you rather than something you either think about or choose.[30]

Adam: This is true of some forms of love, but not all. In my book, I will make a distinction between four ways of loving. I grant that you can't command someone to fall in love. But, you can command other types of love—compassion for example. To "love your neighbors" is to show compassion to them.

Barry: But surely, with compassion there is feeling?

Adam: Of course! All the ways of loving are based in feeling.

Barry: Would you admit that even with compassion you couldn't say: "feel more compassion for your neighbor!" That would be as hard as saying to the young woman, "Fall in love with your friend!"

Adam: True. But, while we have no obligation to fall in love romantically with our friends, we do have a general obligation to act compassionately.

Barry: How so?

Adam: In the great tradition of moral love, compassion rooted in the general human feeling of sympathy, is due to all. It is the most universal of the ways of loving. There is an imperative to act compassionately, to act with kindness, to do good to the Other.

Act II

LOVE'S COMPLEXITY

Scene 1

On the squash court. Adam and Barry play another game and, in between plays, renew their conversation.

Barry: [*disjointedly, with deep breaths in between every few words*] So, you begin with an established tradition of thinking about love. But, I come back to the question of the meaning of love. If you ask a friend, "Do you know what love is?" The likely response will be, "Of course!" If you ask a follow-up question, "Can you explain what love is?" The second response is likely to be less clear. Your friend will probably try to explain love and then become less certain, resorting to analogies, or stories, or say, "Well, if you like someone very much, then it is love. Yet, it's more than that. Sometimes you can love someone and not like him much at all. Moreover, not all loves are the same. I love my cat, but not the same way as I love my partner." You can see the complexity. My worry is this: If love is so complex that explaining it in ordinary speech is difficult for most of us, how can it help us decide how we should live? You told me that for Joseph Fletcher love is the same as a benevolent outcome. Do you agree? Have you anything further by way of a teaser as to what you believe love is?

Adam: I'll give you some broad ideas. Love is one of those primary human experiences that are so foundational that they are conceptually inaccessible.[1]

Barry: [*interrupting*] I don't like the sound of this already!

Adam: [*with exasperation*] If you let me finish! I will go on to say that, even though love is transcategorical, we can identify some attributes that describe it. Yet, to name the attributes is not to exhaust the idea of love.[2] Though love is essentially suprarational—that no conceptual framework is adequate—we speak of it through attributes, through analogy, through metaphor, through story and poetry.

Barry: [*grimacing*] OK, love is conceptually inaccessible, transcategorical, suprarational—but are you going to give me anything concrete!

Adam: I have been drawn to two ideas of Augustine. Love as craving or desire for the object of love, and love as motion toward that object.[3]

Barry: I can understand your first idea: love as desire. That seems straightforward. Plato thought so too. Yet, isn't it true that we desire all manner of things and many of them are not in our best interest. I can see immediately problems for you if you are going to argue for love as a guide to morals and see love rooted in desire. We might develop an inordinate desire for things that are bad for us. We often desire things that belong to others, and that causes all kinds of problems. Desire may lead us to some very difficult places for morality!

Adam: That's true. For love to be a guide to morals, I will suggest that we need to pay particular attention to desire.

Barry: A number of philosophies take desire into account, but often see desire as something problematic. Take Stoicism, for example. The Stoics thought desire was a major obstacle to a well-lived life. In Buddhist philosophy, desire is the root of all suffering. For both the Stoics and Buddhists, a good life would be one free from desires.

Adam: Yes, I am aware of that viewpoint and there is a lot of sense in it. Yet, it strikes me that to be human, in common with all the non-human animals, is to be a being that desires. Desire is rooted in our basic neediness. From the moment of birth we need air, food, water, company, care—the list of needs goes on. Of course, we can desire the bad or the harmful, and we can desire the good or the beneficial. It seems to me that desire, rather than an unfortunate human trait that we need to lose, is a large part of what it means to be human.[4]

Barry: I tend to agree. Needs continue until we die. If desire is closely connected to need, then desire will remain too. But, isn't it true that we often desire far more than we need?

Adam: The problem is not with desire itself, but with the object of our desire. So, even though love is rooted in desire, not all desires have loving outcomes, and not all desires are rooted in love. We need to pay careful attention to what we desire. For instance, for Aristotle, true friendship is one where two friends both desire the good. If friends merely desire what the friend can offer—a kind of quid pro quo—then it is not true friendship.

Barry: You mention desiring the good and seeking the good for the Other. I am going to raise that old philosophical chestnut. [*smiling*] What is the good?

Adam: For Aristotle, the good is that which promotes human flourishing. I would add that human flourishing can only exist where there is love, care, and concern. In other words, the good relates to flourishing and flourishing can only happen in the context of loving relationships. I will have more to say in my book about flourishing in loving relationships as the great good of human life.

Barry: I have more questions about that, but I'll leave it for now.

Adam begins to bounce the ball on his racquet.

Barry: [*grimacing slightly*] You know, your second insight from Augustine may be even more problematic than the first. You say that love is movement from the self toward the Other. In the ancient context, I suspect Augustine was thinking of motion in metaphysical terms. For the ancients, everything was in motion as a fact of being. Objects only appear stationary because an object moving in the opposite direction prevents it from going any further. The ancients thought that all things had such properties as an aspect of their existence, including things such as goodness and truth. For Augustine, love would be a substance in much the same way that we would think of material things. It is not a metaphysics we generally hold to today. So, I assume that if you adopt Augustine's ideas, you will not be speaking of love as a substance.

Adam: That's a good observation. I will be using the idea of motion, or movement, in metaphorical terms rather than in metaphysical terms. In other words, "love is something like movement from one to another."[5]

Barry: That is helpful, though I would rather make an argument in literal terms rather than metaphorical. But for the moment, carry on.

Adam: From my Augustinian insights, I will suggest that love is the feeling, rooted in desire, that draws me from my self to the object of love, the Other, in such a way that through reflection I choose the Good for the Other. In Augustine it is, "*amo: volo ut sis*," I love you, I want you to be." The desire of love is not to merely possess the Other. Love is desire moving through reflection to willed action for the Other's good.[6]

Barry: [*grinning*] Ah, something approaching a definition![7] It's not without its problems, but it will give us something to talk about.

Adam: By the way, in my book, I will capitalize the "Other" and will use it to mean all the others with whom we are in relationships.

Barry: An interesting use. Now carry on.

Adam: Love is very varied: in kind, intensity, in duration. At times, love may be extraordinary pleasurable; at times very painful; and even at times merely mundane. Yet, it is always love *for* the Other. Love is movement toward the forming of relationship. Love is also the longing for relationship, for love is not always satisfied nor consummated in relationship. Love moves from preoccupation with the self to preoccupation with the Other. It is an "un-selfing" for the sake of the Other.[8]

Barry: You realize that you are saying the opposite of Sigmund Freud? He said that love was a "selfing" rather than an un-selfing, where the lover finds herself in the Other.

Adam: Freud's view is interesting and not necessarily contradictory to my view.

Barry: You will need to explain this, because it seems incongruous to me!

Adam: [*patiently*] There is a long tradition that suggests you can only truly find yourself when you lose yourself. A preoccupation with your self and your own needs, to the exclusion of all others, is ultimately destructive to the self. This is because the self is relational rather than isolated. The self in good relationships thrives. The self isolated from others withers. Loneliness is one of the hardest conditions to bear. So, when Freud suggests that in love there is a selfing—a true finding of the self in relationship with the Other—I don't think he is saying anything different.[9]

Barry: What then of your un-selfing?

Adam: In love, there is an un-selfing of the false, isolated self in order to find the true self in relationship with others.

Barry: Let's return to your idea that love is movement toward the Other. Is this true of all love?

Adam: I think so.

Barry: What, then, would you make of the idea of self-love? Isn't self-love very important? It would seem to me to be a kind of love that doesn't move toward the Other, for there is no Other. Yet, surely self-love is still a form of love.

Adam: That's an important issue. To help answer it, let me backtrack a little. In my book, I will try to look at all the common sense ways we use the word love. I'll avoid an approach that defines love so narrowly that many of the ways we speak of love are excluded.

Barry: [*gently pulling his beard*] Ah, yes. Definitions need careful handling. Descriptive definitions are those that tell us what a word means in its everyday usage. A stipulative definition is one where the user imposes a particular meaning. It would go something like this: "When I say love, I mean this and not this."

Adam: Stipulative definitions are quite useful. But sometimes they are overused in that the definition becomes so precise that it bears little resemblance to a descriptive definition. Some scholars have been so keen to stipulate that love is such a lofty ideal that they exclude from true love any way of loving that has some self-benefit. Perhaps the clearest example of this trend was the Swedish scholar Anders Nygren. In his 1953 book, *Agape and Eros*, he drew such a sharp distinction between the two ways of loving in his title that erosic love becomes something less than love.

Barry: [*grimacing a bit*] I recall reading something of his when I was a graduate student. Wasn't his project a religious one?

Adam: Yes. He wanted to show the vast difference between the love of God, agapic love, and love "in the ordinary sense," which is erosic love.[10] He made the gulf so wide that if agapic love is truly love, then erosic love is not.[11]

Barry: And the other way round, I presume?

Adam: Yes. Though scholars who have followed his lead have tended to see agapic love as true love rather than erosic love.

The last point of the day has been played. The two philosophers sit on a bench outside Squash Court 5, absent-mindedly watching the pair playing after them, through the clear glass rear wall of the court.

Barry: So, for Nygren, eros and agape are antithetical. How does Nygren see the difference?

Adam: He makes many distinctions. I will mention just a few to give you the flavor. Eros is acquisitive desire and longing; agape is sacrificial giving. Eros is egocentric love; agape is unselfish love. Eros recognizes value in an object; agape creates value in the object.[12]

Barry: I can see that there are differences in the way we love and experience the love of others, but on the basis of that richness, to exclude some aspects of love seems silly to me. It suggests that what we commonly experience as love is not love at all, but something else, something lower. [*raising an eyebrow*] I do hope you will not take that route in your book?

Adam: No, I won't. Rather than hard dualism—eros is not agape, and therefore only one can be truly called love—I will take a pluralistic view. There are many ways of loving and to call each of them love makes sense in our experience. I will call the first part of my book, "Love's Appearance," in which I will examine the everyday ways we experience and speak of love. For analytical purposes, I will distinguish four ways of loving: erosic love, friendship, affection, and agapic love. In this analysis, I will give something closer to a descriptive rather than a stipulative understanding. I will try my best not to exclude any of the ways we commonly think about love.

Barry: That seems more sensible! So, let me take you back to self-love. Self-love is a common way of speaking about love. Based on what you have said, I can't see how you could exclude it.

Adam: [*interrupting*] However . . .

Barry: There is always a however! I thought this was coming. [*grinning*]

Adam: [*returning a smile*] However, there are occasions in popular speech when we use "love" and we do not mean love. Let me give you an example. [*pausing*] Recently, I was watching a talent show on television.

Barry: Well, I never had you down for that! I am learning all kinds of things about you!

Adam: [*shrugging*] On the show, a young woman had just been selected for the next round by the three judges. She became very excited and started to shout, "I love you! I love you all!" One of the judges replied, "Hold on a minute. You don't love us. You don't even know us. You are just thankful that we put you through to the next round." The judge was telling the singer that she had misappropriated the word love. She was misusing it.

Barry: I'll concede that point. Are you going to tell me that that is what happens when we talk about self-love?

Adam: Sometimes. Self-love is a tricky concept to unpack, but I'll try. At one extreme, self-love has been considered a bad thing. There is a long tradition that you ought to love others before you love yourself. It is the idea behind, [*making quotation marks with his finger in the air*] "selfless service." At the other extreme are views that say every action we take is really a form of self-love. This view tends to say that there is no such thing as altruism. Altruism is disguised self-love.[13]

Barry: Didn't David Hume take issue with that in his day?

Adam: Yes he did, and his argument is still good. He said that to reduce all altruism, benevolence, love, and friendship to self-love is simply contrary to our common feelings on the matter. All animals, including human animals, are susceptible of kindness toward others. He argued for the simplicity of taking disinterested kindness at face value.[14]

Barry: Nonetheless, wouldn't you agree that there is clearly an appropriate kind of self-love that is healthy and enabling for the love of the Other, just as there is a form of self-love that becomes so self-absorbed that others do not count at all?

Adam: Yes. I think we would call that plain selfishness. It reminds me of the myth of Narcissus who was so in love with himself that he perished.[15]

Barry: I don't know many who would agree with mere selfishness as a guide to morals.

Adam: Even Adam Smith, who gave us the idea of enlightened self-interest, suggested that self-interest was moderated by the sentiment of sympathy for others.[16] Yet, ideas change and the pendulum swings. An older view was that you ought to love others before yourself. Nowadays, it is often the reverse: you need to love yourself before you can begin to love others. The idea has become popular in self-help psychologies and has been used to counter the very negative view of the self, derived from certain kinds of religion.[17]

Barry: You mean the religious idea of self-denial?

Adam: Yes, to deny the self in favor of the Other is a very deep thread in the Western psyche and was once part of conventional wisdom. Most considered self-love a moral failing. To love your self first has been a large shift in the popular understanding.

Barry: I agree. Self-help sections of bookstores are full of books urging us to love ourselves. But, I return to my question. Regardless whether this shift has been helpful, it seems to me that self-love is a form of love and that there is no movement from the self to the Other. In your account, self-love can't be love at all.

Adam: It depends what is meant by self-love. In popular usage, self-love often seems to mean something like "accept yourself," or "have some self-worth or self-esteem," or "don't beat yourself up, don't be too hard on yourself." All of those are worthy pieces of advice. Yet, I think there might be a misapplication of the word love.

Barry: How so?

Adam: Why use self-love when we actually mean self-acceptance? Acceptance and love are not the same. If you mean "self-worth," why not simply say so rather than self-love?

Barry: So, in those cases, "self-love" is misapplied.

Adam: Yes. But that is a minor issue. More importantly, I worry that much self-love talk might be thinly disguised selfishness. "Look after number one, and forget about others." Some scholars have noticed a change in contemporary society from "other-regardingness" to "self-regardingness." This social change correlates with a loss of what Robert Bellah called the "habits of the heart."[18] These habits were often directed toward the Other.

Barry: You know, of course, that a correlation does not indicate a cause. Self-regardingness might not be caused by an emphasis in popular psychology on self-love, but it's an interesting thought nonetheless. [*frowning, and thinking for a while*] Let me try to summarize: First, you said that love is movement from the self to the Other. Second, you said that you are going to use everyday understandings and experiences of love. Third, I responded that self-love is an everyday use of the word love, but there is no movement of the self-to the Other. Fourth, you responded that sometimes self-love is a misuse of the word love, when we mean something else, like self-acceptance. Agreed?

Adam: Agreed!

Barry: But not every use of self-love is a misuse of the word love? So, you think there is an appropriate self-love?

Adam: Yes.

Barry: Explain to me then how self-love can be love when there is no movement toward an Other.

Adam: Let me remind you that "love as movement toward the Other" is metaphor. When we speak of self-love we say, "I love myself." It is as if the "I" and the "Self" are two, not one. The Self is the object loved by the subject "I."

Barry: You're not suggesting that everyone has a dual personality are you?

Adam: Not at all! Yet, the way we try to make sense of our consciousness is often to speak as if consciousness can be divided. Its duality surfaces in different contexts when we speak of the true self and the false self, or the inner self and the outer self, or the real self and the socially constructed self.

Barry: You mean something like Carl Jung's "ego and "self,"[19] Or R. D. Laing's "true self and false self"?[20]

Adam: Yes. Or like the early theologian, Paul of Tarsus' two "I's" in his letter to the Roman Christians.[21] These are ways of trying to make sense of what it means to be a self-conscious person. The self can be the object of self-consciousness. I can think about my self. I is the subject, and self is the object as I think about myself. I can do so with hatred or with some affection. It fits the subject/object criterion—or better subject/subject criterion—the movement of the self to the Other.

Barry: So, are you saying that there is movement in self-consciousness that might be called love?

Adam: Yes. That would be the way I would make sense of the concept of self-love. I think self-love is necessary preparation for moral actions. As M.

Scott Peck suggested, we are a part of humanity, and if we are to love humanity, we need to love ourselves.

Barry: I have always found that a reasonable way to think of self-love. It seems strange to me that you could loath yourself yet love others. It was the self-deprecation of religion that turned me off as much as philosophical issues about belief in God.

Adam: I tend to agree. Yet, there is something fundamentally moral about the act of un-selfing.[22] Un-selfing and self-love are not mutually exclusive. In moral terms, it is this un-selfing, this focus on the Other, which makes love a fitting basis for the moral life. When self-love becomes primary with no connectedness outside of the self, when there is no movement toward the Other, and no forming of relationship, then self-love is pure selfishness. True self-love (in the sense of the love of self as a part of love of humanity) would be movement from the false self (self-centeredness) to the true self in relationship with the Other. With love, there is a community of selves.

Scene 2

Half an hour later in the locker room, Barry and Adam gather their bags, checking around the central benches for anything left behind. Both have wet hair from the shower. Both are still red-faced from the exertion of the games.

Barry: So, let me see if I understand you clearly. You suggest love is an affect, rooted in desire, that seeks the good for the Other. This involves the lover in a movement (metaphorically speaking) toward the Other.

Adam: That's close! But I don't want to begin with a definition. The father of existentialism, Søren Kierkegaard, wrote a wonderful book called *The Works of Love*. You might say the book was about what love looks like in action. I want to take a leaf from Kierkegaard's book and look at love not by trying to say what love is, but what love looks like in its effects.[23]

Barry: I see. [*frowning slightly*] Something like, I can't define love for you, but I can show you what it looks like.

Adam: Yes, that's the kind of thing. In my book I take that approach. So when I ask what love looks like, my answer is, "Love looks like romance and sexual love; love looks like deep friendships; love looks like affection; and love looks like compassion and altruism. Love is many faceted."

Adam and Barry leave the locker room. After walking in silence for a while they continue the discussion.

Adam: Besides being a noble tradition of thought and practice, love addresses our existential reality as what Aristotle called social animals[24]—though I prefer to say relational rather than social.

Barry: Why's that?

Adam: I think it's a broader term. "Social" in social and political philosophy generally refers to relationships between human beings in a traditional humanistic, political sense. I want to expand the idea and say that human beings relate to more than other human beings, though of course, human relationships are foundational. We relate to other sentient beings, often in profound ways. Loving concern is expansive and includes love for non-human animals.

Barry: I certainly love my little pug Jack!

Adam: I would also extend loving relationship to non-living things. The love of beauty is relational, as is the love of music, to give only two examples. Of course, it is not reciprocally relational. Nonetheless, it makes sense to talk, say, of a love of art.

Barry: Hmm. Can you explain why the relational is an important aspect of morality?

Adam: To speak of ethics in any way other than social, or in my terms relational, makes little sense to me. Our "shoulds" always refer to relationship with the Other.

Barry: I must raise a red flag! I need to hear you carefully, but you might be in danger of doing injustice to a central tenet of modern ethical thought: that of the autonomous individual. Surely, the concept of human autonomy, respect for the individual person, is itself a moral concept. The notion of "self-rule" and a "good will"—the freedom to choose the right course of action—is well established in Kant. And that does not involve a relationship with any Other.

Adam: Of course, I agree that the concept of personal autonomy is essential. But, if you mean moral life only concerns individual moral actors and their radically free choice, then, I dissent. Morality is always deeply personal, yet always more than personal. I would say, "interpersonal," or "relational."

Barry: Can you explain what you mean?

Adam: Quite simply, the idea of the solitary individual who lives without reference to others doesn't square with lived experience. Aristotle was correct: we are social beings. Our personal choices affect others. I find it very hard to think of an action that is merely personal.

Barry: Let's test this out.

Adam: By all means!

Barry: Let's think about euthanasia. The debate is about a personal decision to choose to end one's life. Surely, that is about human autonomy and is purely personal.

Adam: But euthanasia is not merely personal. It's a choice that affects the Other—be that family, acquaintances, or medical staff, and all who are concerned with the patient.

Barry: In most cases, I agree with you. But surely, what makes euthanasia a moral issue is that it is about the personal choice of the individual. Individual choices about your own body matter as moral issues.

Adam: You have simply turned the issue around. What you choose to do with your own body is a personal matter. Insofar as your choices affect others, it is a moral matter. Yet, the discussion about euthanasia as you framed it is whether I, or we as a society, or anyone, ought to respect your personal decisions. My respecting your decisions is a relational issue, and hence, in my terms an ethical issue.

Barry: I can imagine a situation of the lone individual, who has no relations or friends—who literally knows no one—who chooses to commit suicide. Isn't that purely personal?

Adam: If such a situation were possible, then I suppose so—though it would be a very sad tale to tell. Even then, there are questions of who will dispose of the body, and what to do with the person's belongings. There would also likely be a coroner's report. So, at the very least, these post-death costs would be borne by someone. Because of the complexity of the web of interactions, I find it difficult to think of personal choices that affect only the individual. Take, for example, consumer purchases. On a trip to the local shopping mall, you buy a pair of sneakers. The decision affects only you. No one else is concerned about the decision; no one else will wear the sneakers. Yet, when you consider the way the sneakers are made, the people affected in the production process, the capitalistic system that affects many people, environmental factors from industrial production—the list goes on and on—then, it is clear that the simple act of buying the shoes is a moral choice. It would also be the case that the purchase of sneakers would mean that money would not be available for other purchases. If there were dependents—family members—it is clear that consumer purchases affect others.

Barry: I still want to press into this further. I am trying to think of a choice that is purely personal. What of the personal act of masturbation? Historically, self-pleasuring has been considered a moral action (usually an immoral one). Of all the things people do, surely this is the most personal and affects no other.

Adam: I will stick my neck out and go against the centuries of moralizing about masturbation. Most of the time masturbation is an amoral action. That is, morality does not enter the picture. I am presupposing, of course, that the act only affects the individual performing it.

Barry: [*pausing*] So, do I hear you correctly: morality only comes into play when a personal choice or action affects the Other?

Adam: Yes, [*with hesitation*] I would say that. Why do I feel something is just about to come around the corner?

Barry: [*mischievously*] Well, let me introduce God to our discussion.

Adam: [*grinning*] An unusual move for you!

Barry: Though I find no use for God myself, there is a long tradition that sees morality as living in accordance with the will of God—divine command theory as it's often called. God commands moral actions and people are supposed to obey. If people disobey, then God is displeased. Surely, for theists, God is the supreme Other. Because God is always watching, I presume, every action affects God. As God is the Other, then it would fit your category of a moral action. When I was a boy, in my religion class [*wryly smiling*] I was told that God forbids masturbation. It made God upset. It was a very bad thing to do.

Adam: In that respect, your religion teachers had a great deal in common with Immanuel Kant.

Barry: Yes, he was rather an absolutist about masturbation.[25] He compared it to suicide and condemned both actions. Yet, he considered suicide as preferable. At least suicide takes courage! [*laughing*]

Adam: I would just observe that ancient religious texts are ambiguous. Some say that there are sacred texts that proscribe masturbation.[26] These texts tend to be ones that decry "spilling seed," and are in the context of ensuring the production of the next generation in primitive agricultural communities. I don't know of any specific "thou shalt not masturbate" commandments. So, even for those who want to accept divine command theory, the divine commands in this instance are not clear. Nonetheless, if someone truly thinks what they are doing offends God it can have profound psychological affect—usually with complex layers of guilt. It would be an interesting avenue to explore, but in my book, I will stay with my idea that morality proper relates to human relationships mostly with other human beings, but also with sentient non-human animals and with the environment that affects sentient life. For the most part, I will leave God out of the moral equation.

Barry: I'm not sure I'm going to let you! What I am saying is that if you are a religious person, then no action is merely personal because God is always there as well. I must say again that as I have no use for God, I can imagine merely personal issues. But, as you are a theist, is that your view: the ever-watchful God, commanding morality, then watching to see if we fail?

Adam: Not really. My theism is more properly termed "panentheism." I long ago abandoned the rather simple metaphor of God "up there and our there . . ."

Barry: [*interrupting*] "Way beyond the blue . . ." [*singing along to an old song*]

Adam: [*smiling broadly*] Panentheism is the concept that God is at once transcendent and immanent; the ultimately real beyond anything we could imagine or name, and yet intimately connected—in interbeing some Buddhists would say—to all that is. God is in all and all is in God.

Barry: Isn't that pantheism? Everything is God?

Adam: Panentheism is a little different, in that whilst God is in all that is, God is also beyond all that is.

Barry: Sounds something like Plotinus's "the One," and not unlike Daoism, where the dao is in all that is, yet as Laozi says, "The dao that can be named is not the true Dao."

Adam: It is the most common understanding of God in all the world's great mystical traditions. Aldous Huxley called it "The Perennial Philosophy."[27]

Barry: [*grimacing slightly*] Does that effect ethics in any way, or is it all metaphysical ramblings?

Adam: In that great tradition, more often than not, the Ultimately Real is perceived as love, and as all things will ultimately resolve to the One, then love becomes a central goal. Also, thinking back to our discussion about self-love, in the mystical tradition the love of self-love is love of the divine within.

Scene 3

Later in the cafe/bar of the sports center, Barry and Adam are re-hydrating with fruit juice and Perrier water.

Adam: [*picking up in the middle of their conversation*] . . . I still don't think it was a let. I really couldn't have reached the ball.

Barry: Well, you know squash is a game for gentlefolk. [*smiling*] Besides, I would rather err on the side of generosity. I would have been troubled if we didn't replay the point. Besides, I still won! The gods were smiling on me.

Adam: But you don't believe in gods!

Barry: [*laughing*] Fair enough! [*sipping his drink*] Can we return to clarify how your account of love as a guide to morals differs from traditional deontology, consequentialism, and virtue? Can you say more?

Adam: I think it is not as simple to separate duty and consequences. If I am to love my child, my love will be mindful of the kinds of consequences my actions toward my child will have. If love is a guide to morals, then my love will act on obligations and consider consequences. I will only do so in so far as I have developed loving character traits. So, I don't want to be bound by a strict categorization. It is not a case of being either a deontologist or a utilitarian or a virtue ethicist. Each of those ways of looking at morality plays a part.

Barry: Examples?

Adam: In the tradition of moral love, it is clear that love is enjoined as an obligation—the primary human duty. Spouses have the duty to love each other—at least, traditional vows say so. Parents have a duty to love their children. In other words love is deontological. Love is the guiding principle by which we should act. Yet, love is also teleological. In seeking to love, we must be mindful of the consequences of actions. The moral task is to take those actions that will have the most loving outcomes. By the same token, love is a virtue. Those people will seek to love—both as duty and as mindful of consequences—will need to develop the virtue of love, to become a loving person. And a loving person will most likely make the most loving decisions.

Barry: An interesting point—though I'm not convinced that loving people always make the most loving decisions. Love can blind people to decisions that have the most loving outcomes. A little boy comes home from school with a tale of bullying. His mother loves the little boy so much she is incensed and fearful, and wants to rush out and fix things. However, if she does so she may make things worse in the long run for the boy. She is clearly a loving person, but that does not translate into the most loving decisions.

Adam: That is true, and helps clarify my point. A loving disposition is inadequate alone, as is a sense of duty alone or a consideration of consequences alone. It is why deontology needs teleology and both need virtue for a helpful moral perspective. In fact, I will devote the third part of my book to looking at love's practice—the virtues and habits of love—that shapes the disposition of a loving person.

Barry: That sounds like an Aristotelian argument.

Adam: Well observed! Rather than look at ethics as a system of rules to be followed, it is a practice of life to be engaged in. In my terms, an ethical life is one that consists of love as a practice.

Barry: I hear echoes of Alasdair MacIntyre in the notion of practice.

Adam: [*taking a drink of juice*] Yes, I owe a great deal to MacIntyre's renewed Aristotelianism. He wrote a very important book in 1981—*After Virtue*. It was a critique of Enlightenment moral philosophy and suggested that philosophers reconsider Aristotle. It caused quite a stir with much debate about whether he had understood the Enlightenment correctly. Regardless of that debate, the long lasting effect of his work was to get many to reconsider Aristotle. My book will be in some ways an outworking of MacIntyre's suggestion. Though I doubt he would have taken it the way I do.

Barry: To return to your suggestion that love as a guide to morals is deontological, consequentialist, and virtue-based all at the same time, can you give me another example? I want to be sure I am hearing you correctly.

Adam: Let's take an example from the way of loving we call friendship. The principle of seeking your friend's best interests is a part of what friendship means. If you are my friend, to be a good and loving friend to you, I should seek your best interests. To become a friend is to take on that obligation. Would you agree?

Barry: Of course!

Adam: One day, I hear that someone on the faculty is spreading an untrue rumor about something you are supposed to have said about the Dean.

Barry: [*smiling wryly*] Surely there would be no truth in such a rumor! [*slyly winking*]

Adam: Of course! But what am I to do with the information I now have? For the sake of friendship, I have a duty to do that which I consider in your best interest. Yet, I can't do that without thinking about possible consequences.

Barry: Ah, so here duty and consequences converge.

Adam: Yes. I can choose to say nothing. The consequences might be that the tittle-tattle blows over and there are no further repercussions. Or, it might get out of hand with reputations damaged. Or I could choose to tell you, and risk you feeling personally hurt that a colleague might malign you through busy-bodying. Yet, you might then be able to do something about it for your long-term good.

Barry: You could also leave me out completely and confront the offending faculty member yourself. It might be risky to you—you might upset that person, they may turn on you—who knows? If you resolved the issue, then I could carry merrily along oblivious to the whole affair.

Adam: I'm sure there are other possible consequences of the various actions. My point is a simple one. Even if I considered myself bound by the duties of friendship, I could only do that adequately by thinking through the consequences for your well-being. Further, neither duty nor consequences would matter much unless I had developed the personal character traits that enabled me to act on my obligations.

Barry: So, that is how you add virtue to obligations and consequences?

Adam: Yes.

Barry: [*shaking his head*] By your lights, love is complex! I will raise one more issue before we go home. It sounds to me that your version of love as a guide to morals is very situationist. Loving actions in diverse contexts, given similar moral dilemmas, might be different. Am I right?

Adam: Yes. Take truth telling as an example. We know from experience that telling the truth, in more cases than not, is a more loving action than telling lies, and so we can adopt a rule that generally speaking, it will be the more loving thing to tell the truth than to lie. However, the general rule is not set in concrete as, at times, to not tell the truth—by omitting something or by telling a direct lie—may be more loving. There is a general principle, yet the principle is subject to the context of particular situations when the principle may be abandoned.

Barry: So, the principle of maximizing loving outcomes, wherever possible, trumps the rule that you should always tell the truth.

Adam: Yes. Generally, love would tell the truth for the sake of the integrity of the Other. But on occasion, love might demand that a lie be told for the sake of the Other. Love as a guide to morals is situational, yet rooted in general principles that we know tend toward loving outcomes.

Barry: This sounds like rule utilitarianism. Given similar situations, similar decisions produce similar pleasure. We then make a general rule that says, "If you do this, you will produce this amount of pleasure and this amount of pain." It proves to be the case that because so many of our actions are so similar, we don't have to make a "utility calculation" for every act. We know from experience that certain types of action will generally bring more pleasure than pain and so we can adopt a rule for it. Would not love be the same?[28]

Adam: For some actions, I agree. Yet, I want to call those loving responses to similar situations principles rather than rules.[29] Principles allow for exceptions in a way that rules do not.

Barry: [*a little irritated*] That might be splitting hairs! [*pausing*] Let me ask one more issue that's puzzling me. I can imagine a situation where two people face the same moral dilemma and yet differ in their conclusion. Let's say that they are equally loving people who want to reach the most loving outcome. Wouldn't they need something other than love to act as an arbitrator between them—something like rules to follow in a deadlock situation? And if so, then love cannot be the guide to morals that you want it to be.

Adam: I can imagine that too! I would go further and say that this is most likely to be the case. To say that love is a guide to morals is not to provide a watertight answer to every moral issue. Love is not an easy answer. But then, no serious moral prescription is. To prioritize love reminds us that the best solution will be a loving solution, that we have a duty, therefore, to seek loving solutions to moral issues, and that loving solutions require loving people.

Barry: Isn't that all a bit ambiguous?

Adam: I can live with that. Life is ambiguous.

Barry: I must say that I'm looking forward to our continued discussion. I know you're a fan of Iris Murdoch. Didn't she say something about the task of philosophy being to uncover obvious issues that are often hidden? I hope you can do that . . . But right now, I'm ready for home, my favorite chair, and a cup of tea.[30]

Act III

LOVE'S APPEARANCE: EROS

Scene 1

In the Senior Common Room where faculty members relax between classes, drink coffee or hot chocolate from a machine and catch up with each other's news. Around half a dozen faculty members are milling around.

Barry: [*taking a Styrofoam cup from the drink dispenser, spilling the contents a little*] Why does this machine always give you too much! Surely, it would be a simple matter to adjust.

Faculty member [*from the back of the room, in a loud voice*] Someone needs to tell someone. Barry, are you going to?

Barry: [*in an equally loud voice*] Probably not! So we'll just have to keep scalding ourselves and complaining! [*turning to Adam, more quietly*] I've a few minutes. May we talk about your book again?

Adam: Of course! Though I've got a class in ten minutes. What's on your mind?

Barry: You have given me something of an understanding of love—as rooted in desire and as movement toward the Other. You have given me a glimpse of what love looks like in action. We have explored some of the complexities in even speaking about love. You have said that your argument is a type of Aristotelian argument. Can you explain more?

Adam: My argument will not be Aristotelian in the sense that Aristotle made the same argument. For instance, he had no place for love as altruistic. His was very much a masculinist, aristocratic philosophy. He had no place for women at all and no place for men who were not of his social standing. Needless to say, Aristotle was a product of his culture, and the cultured elite in his day shared his viewpoint. From our point of view, we would strongly criticize Aristotle's elitism.

Barry: Agreed. But, my guess is that you want to find something positive in Aristotle and not "throw out the baby with the bath water"?[1]

Adam: Yes, some specific ways of thinking can be abstracted from Aristotle that are very useful. My argument will have a methodology derived from the Aristotelian tradition as interpreted by Alasdair MacIntyre.

Barry: [*laughing*] Your interpretation of Alasdair MacIntyre's interpretation of Aristotle! It does get complicated! How will you work this out?

Adam: MacIntyre argues that Aristotle characterized the ethical life in this way: first, untutored human-nature-as-it-happens-to-be; second, human-nature-as-it-could-be-if-it-realized-its telos; and finally, rational ethics as means to transition from the first to the second.[2]

Barry: That's a reasonable interpretation. May I ask for clarification of a few things. [*pausing to take a sip of his hot drink*] You use the Greek word telos. By that I assume you mean the goal toward which something is moving. In Aristotle, this was a matter of nature. All things have a natural telos. The acorn has its telos in the oak tree. The acorn has potentiality, but has not realized its natural purpose until it is the mature tree.

Adam: That's a good observation. For Aristotle, the telos of human life was eudaimonia. The word usually means "happiness," but it is more than mere feelings of happiness. Aristotle meant well-being in the widest possible sense. Human flourishing is a good way to say it. Life as it happens to be (for Aristotle) is less than flourishing. If human life reached its telos, it would be a life of the utmost well-being. To move from one to the other requires the development of the virtues that make for a eudemonic life.

Barry: You're right; for Aristotle the telos meant a life of happiness in its fullest sense. Any person who has not yet achieved that eudemonic life has not yet achieved her telos. Are you taking this Aristotelian idea as it stands?[3]

Adam: No. I will suggest a modification of Aristotle's understanding of telos. I agree with you that he assumed that all things have a natural telos. That acorns have the natural telos of oak trees seems perfectly fine. Yet, the analogy breaks down when we consider human beings. I find it hard to think of human beings having a natural telos. Our ability to choose goals and to make decisions about what we want to achieve makes the idea of a natural goal problematic. In my book, I will use a notion I have developed that I call an "elective teleology." By that, I mean simply that a natural telos is not given to human beings, but we can choose a telos for our lives.

Barry: I am glad you have said that, because I have always found the Aristotelian idea of purpose problematic. It is not clear to me that even acorns have a telos. A purpose suggests some kind of agency; some mind that formulates the purpose. I think that is why Thomas Aquinas, in the thirteenth century, so easily adapted Aristotle to Christianity. He blended Augustinian theology with Aristotelian philosophy. Being a theist, Aquinas thought that the agency, or the mind behind the purpose of the world—and all things in the world—was God. Being an atheist, I have always found it hard to accept that there is any purpose or telos to life—

by that, I mean a natural purpose given to life. Purpose, or goal, requires agency. Acorns and oak trees do not have agency. People do, and your idea of an elective telos is interesting.

Adam: [*smiling broadly*] I'm amazed that you agree!

Barry: If a telos can be chosen, what would you choose? (Though I can imagine the answer from our conversation so far.)

Adam: I would choose love as the telos of human life.

Barry: [*laughing*] Surprise! Surprise!

Adam: In answer to my original question, "How should we live?" I answer, "We should aim for a loving life—make love our goal." So, my modification of the Aristotelian ethical argument is this: human life, as it happens to be in its untutored form, is often less than loving. To choose love as the telos of human life would suggest to us what life could be like. The moral life would be one of movement from a less loving life to a more loving life. The way to achieve that would be to build loving habits that become loving virtues (a loving character), which make up the practice of love. It is in that Aristotelian sense that love is a guide to morals.

Barry: So, let me be clear. You appear to adopt a framework that is similar to Aristotle's. Yet, the in your position is that you make love the telos rather than eudaimonia.

Adam: Yes. I will say that human thriving is a noble telos. Yet, eudaimonia can only be realized in loving relationships. I will use Aristotle's own insight that human beings are social animals.

Barry: Tell me more about how you will work this out.

Adam: My book will have three parts: love's appearance, love-itself, and love's practice. Love's appearance will deal with love as it happens to be in our everyday experience. Presently, we know love in many diverse, yet imperfect ways. Love in our day-to-day experience is profoundly good, yet mixed. Second, love-itself will deal with love as we could imagine it more perfectly. I ask the question: what would love be like if unmixed?

Barry: An ideal of love?

Adam: Yes. I call this love-itself. Love-itself is the highest aspiration and desire of humanity as relational beings. Finally, I will deal with love's practice and look particularly at the habits and virtues of love.

Barry: [*pausing in thought*] Hmm. Love-itself. That sounds as though it might be hyphenated.

Adam: You know me too well! In my book, as you say, "love-itself" will be hyphenated. I am borrowing from the existentialists' use of the device. For example, Jean-Paul Sartre's "for-itself," and "in-itself," and Martin Buber's "I-Thou," and "I-It." In the ethics of care, Nel Noddings uses "one-caring" and "one-cared-for." They are all good precedents.[4]

Barry: It's a useful mechanism in that a basic concept does not need an explanation each time it is used. Still, I'm not fond of it. But, for me it's a minor point. [*pausing*] You speak of love's appearance. Tell me how you are using the term "appearance." There is a long philosophical tradition of different connotations here. Many have tried to consider the difference between what is *really* the case and what only *appears* to be the case.

Adam: Aristotle suggested that it's best to begin with "appearances"—how the world strikes us in our everyday lives. This is about the way we perceive the world around us as well as about our ordinary beliefs about it. Appearances are how we make sense of the world.

Barry: You might want to consider Max Weber and his *Sociology of Religion.*[5] This was his methodology too. He promised a definition of religion, but only after he had given many instances of what religion looks like in practice—that is, how it appears to us. His, too, was an Aristotelian approach. You'll recall that he died before finishing the book and never gave the definition. Yet, mid-way through the book, we didn't need one because it had become clear. So, your method is well tried and a good one.

Adam: Kant also speaks of appearances. For him, it was impossible to know a "thing-in-itself."[6] We can only ever know how something appears to us. Kant called what is really the case the noumenon. What appears to be the case he called the phenomenon. He used this method in his *Critique of Practical Reason.*[7] Nowhere does he tell us what practical reason is in-itself, but gives instead many instances of how practical reason is perceived.

Barry: So, if you follow Kant, you will not be able to say anything about love-itself because love itself is unknowable!

Adam: In part, that is true. When I say, "love's appearance" I am thinking of the phenomenal in the Kantian sense: love as perceived in our experience. When I speak of love-itself, I will be thinking of love in the Kantian noumenal sense.

Barry: Then I repeat, you can't say anything about love-itself! [*rubbing his chin*] I'm confused.

Adam: In my book, I will use the argument from perfection similar to that used by Iris Murdoch. I will argue that it is the imagining of love-itself—the noumenon, the perfect love, the ideal—that helps us see how we should live better lives. Contemplation of the good has a long tradition in philosophy. But, remember, I don't begin with the contemplation of the perfect; I begin with the appearance of love. That is essential to my method. May I bring us back to that?

Barry: Of course!

Adam: I begin by casting a glance at the kinds of love that we experience in our everyday lives. By examining what appears to be the case about love, we might be able to have a broader grasp of what we generally mean by love. I will map the experiences of love, both in our perceptions and in our basic and common beliefs. Then, having mapped out the way love appears, I will look at love's appearance through the lens of love-itself. Finally, I will suggest love's practice that will help us move from one toward the other. I move from everyday experience, to contemplation and analysis, and then to practice, that, in turn, informs and shapes experience.

Barry: It will be interesting to see how you make these connections. But, something has been bothering me. Love in our experience is often a very mixed affair. It can be delightfully fulfilling. It can be desperately destructive. I am not sure how you will be able to use our mixed experience of love as a guide to morals.

Adam: I will argue that the loves we experience are often misapplied-loves, misdirected-loves, corrupted-loves, and immature-loves. Sometimes what we call love is not love at all. At times, our love may be directed toward the wrong object—say, the adult who sexually loves the child. Often, our loves contain an admixture of something other than love that corrupts love. Even at their best, our loves imperfectly reflect the maturity of love-itself.

Scene 2

A few hours later. Adam, walking down the corridor with classrooms on each side, notices students filing out of Room G202. This is Barry's class. Adam looks inside and sees Barry vigorously cleaning the chalkboard, clouds of dust filling the front of the room. The winter sunlight through the window highlights the dust in the air. Adam enters.

Adam: [*laughing*] You know I have never seen anyone clean a board with such gusto! It's a wonder you don't choke yourself. Anyway, who uses a chalkboard anymore?

Barry: [*turning to see Adam*] You're not the first to accuse me of being a Luddite. The old methods are tried and tested.

Adam: [*grinning broadly*] So back to our conversation. [*pausing*] I make a general assumption that we have at least a rudimentary experience of love and . . .

Barry: [*interrupting*] Slow down a bit! I was little worried earlier when you said, "love in our everyday experience," but I let it go. Now I must stop you. I am always a little suspicious when the words "our" or "we" are used. Often, it assumes far too much. It lumps everyone together, as if the human experience is always the same. I'm not so sure it is. May I explain?

Adam: Of course!

Barry: We can't assume that there is homogeneity of people. "We" and "us" are problematic ideas. Dominant groups often assume that others share their experiences—the dominant perspective of the world. Too often they use "us," and the "us" excludes so many. Just look at the way men have historically used the "we" and have excluded not only women, but also men of color and, often, poor men.

Adam: [*frowning with irritation*] Of course, I agree. But, at the same time, wouldn't you agree that there must be at least the beginnings of commonality or language is meaningless.

Barry: Carry on.

Adam: If I say, "It's a warm day," you may answer, "Too hot for me!" We have a conversation that is meaningful because we have the common experience of warm days in the past. We might have disagreements about what amounts to too hot and what amounts to just right, but our common experience gives us a starting place.

Barry: Granted.

Adam: Love is like that. It seems to me that there is a common human experience of love. It may be stronger or more fulfilling for different people. It will probably vary in intensity over time. For some, it will be a fleeting moment, and for others, it may last a lifetime. Yet, it would be a very sad and deprived person who had not known at least some measure of love at some point in life. The fact that we can say "love" and have at least the beginning of understanding of each other supports my assertion. I would go so far as to say that the fact that anyone is alive is prima facie evidence that they have known love—at least in its most rudimentary form of parental care. If there is no common experience of what we call love, then we can't even begin a conversation. Will you allow me that?[8]

Barry: Yes, except for those with a severe pathology such as reactive attachment disorder.[9] Though few and far between, there are those who have known no love. That aside, can you give me an example to make your point clear?

Adam: Let's say I come 'round to your home for an evening of relaxation over a glass or two of wine.

Barry: Sounds inviting!

Adam: As I enter, your little dog Jack waddles over wagging his tail. You shout him over and he leaps onto your lap. You wouldn't need to say so, but I know you love your little dog. It's in your manner, your face. I can see it without you saying anything.

Barry: Yes, I do love him, the little rascal!

Adam: In part, I know it because I also love my dog. There is a commonality about our love. If you were to say to me, "I love Jack," I would know pretty much what you mean. I have shared the love of animal companionship. Our loves may not be of the same intensity. Yet, there is the beginning of shared understanding from the commonality of our experiences. Now, not everyone shares such loves, but it is such a common experience that I think I can confidently talk about the shared affection we have for animals.

Barry: You've got me on a soft spot! So let's agree for the moment that there is some commonality about our experience. Carry on with your argument and let's see where it leads.

Adam: When looking at love's appearance, I will make a distinction between "self-regarding love" and "other-regarding love." The distinction is based on the question, "for whose sake is the love?" Some loves are clearly more about the person doing the loving than the person or thing loved. When we say in popular speech, "I love chocolate," the loving is not for the sake of the chocolate at all. That kind of love is about the desire of the lover and the enjoyment that comes from possession of the Other. Yet, when a mother loves her child, the love is more often for the sake of the child and its well-being.

Barry: But, isn't love a little more of a mixed bag than that? The mother who loves her child receives something back: the joy of parenthood, the satisfaction of a child doing well at school, and, perhaps most importantly, the child's love in return.

Adam: I agree. That is part of the complexity of love. Parental love is both other-regarding and self-regarding. It fulfills the need of the parent, yet is a gift to the child.

Barry: You mention needs. I think it's true that much human behavior is a response to motivational needs. That concept has been developed well in education and in management theories. I have tended to think of love as directly related to the needs of the lover and the one loved.

Adam: You are thinking of something like Abraham Maslow's Hierarchy of Needs,[10] and I will have a discussion in my book about his ideas. His theory is usually presented as a pyramid, with physiological needs at the base—food, water and such. There are then subsequent levels of safety needs, such as security and employment. Then belonging needs—meaning family, friends, and those close to you. Then there are the needs of self-esteem, respect, and similar things. Finally, there are self-actualizing needs, including morality, creativity, and other similar needs. Placing a focus on human need is a good one. We seek loving relationships because we have a need to. Yet, our love of the Other is also directed at meeting "their" needs.

Barry: Needs *are* fascinating.

Adam: Yes, but I would place higher value on what Maslow called "belongingness needs." These were the emotional needs of love and affection. While they were mid-positioned in his hierarchy, I'd place them as the highest aspirations of humanity.

Barry: Why is that?

Adam: Maslow's view is rooted too deeply in a post-Enlightenment view of the individual. Before the modern period—hard though it is for us to think about it—people thought more in community, family, or other collective ways. The individuality of the person was subsumed under social roles. The Enlightenment changed our ways of thinking. We have become much more used to thinking that an individual is separate from and can transcend any social role. As a result, many folks in our culture have become somewhat disconnected. The isolated individual who can rise above relationships to fulfill loftier needs is part of the problem and not the solution.

Barry: [*smiling*] Why I am not surprised at your interpretation?

Adam: Nonetheless, I appreciate a needs-based approach. However, I would say that not all love is based in needs. C. S. Lewis looked at this and made a distinction between "need-love," "gift-love," and "appreciative love." He recognized that all human beings are a bundle of needs and that one of those needs—the chief psychological need—is love. There's nothing wrong with that. To need is integral to our humanity.[11]

Barry: I'm reminded of the interesting Greek myth where Zeus splits the original human being—a man-woman—into man and woman to curb their turbulence. Since then, we are all looking for the one to make us complete again. We are lonely and lost until we find the other half of ourselves. It's a quaint story![12]

Adam: I love those myths! But, with Lewis, I don't think all love is based on the drive to fulfill personal needs. A mother loves her child, often, for the sake of the child. That is other-regarding-love.

Barry: Though, even here you could argue that the maternal instinct is a need to love the child.

Adam: You could. But, sometimes we love something and it meets neither a need in us nor a need in the object of love. It is merely deep appreciation, wonder, even worship.

Barry: We spoke before of those scholars, such as Nygren, who have made the suggestion that the purest form of love has no self-regard at all.

Adam: I will look at it further when I consider love-itself. I will argue that love-itself is other-regarding, self-regarding, and appreciative. I do not consider need-love as something less than the other two. The highest relationships are reciprocal, and need-love and gift-love are both essential in the forming of relationships. In fact, some scholars suggest that there must be reciprocation for love to be love.[13] I would not go that far. I may love you, even though you do not love me back. Though reciprocation might be the goal, there is always the risk that love will remain unrequited.

Barry: Good! I doubt that pure altruism is even possible, other than in theory. In that, I'm a skeptic.

Adam: Perhaps, we can talk about that later. I've got a curriculum meeting. It should only be an hour or so. I'll pop by your office and see if you're still here when I'm finished.

Scene 3

Adam's meeting goes on longer than anticipated. He arrives breathless at the Philosophy Department having almost jogged across campus, anxious not to miss Barry. He finds Barry chatting with Lucy, a senior philosophy student.

Barry: [*to Lucy, with a nod in Adam's direction*] Ah! The wanderer returns! (*to Adam*) I bet Lucy will be interested in your book Adam.

Lucy: Absolutely! I'm always up for a good read. What's it about? It won't be above my head, will it?

Adam: Not at all! It's an argument about love as a guide to morals.

Lucy: Sounds fascinating. Though I doubt I'll have much to add. But, I'd love to hear more about it.

Barry: We're just going to chat about it now. Listen in if you wish.

Lucy: Thanks!

Adam and Barry and Lucy pull up chairs close to the desk.

Barry: [*turning to Adam*] Explain more fully your Aristotelian argument.

Adam: When looking at love's appearance I will make it clear that our experiences of love are quite complex. To help steer a clear course I will speak of four ways of loving.

Barry: How did you settle on four? I have heard of two kinds of love—using the Greek words agape and eros, usually translated as altruism or compassion, and sexual love.

Adam: Yes, that is a popular way to think about love. Some philosophers add a third—usually *philia*, or friendship—and Robert Wagoner even finds six kinds of love.[14] With C. S. Lewis, who wrote *The Four Loves*, I will speak of four. However, I am not speaking of different loves (as he seems to), but ways of loving. I think love is "one," but love is expressed in different ways.

Barry: What, then, are your four ways of loving?

Adam: Erosic love, friendship, affection, and agapic love.

Barry: I have two immediate questions. It may not be obvious to your readers what erosic and agapic mean. What not use more familiar words? And, is the order important?

Adam: To answer your first question, erosic love is a way of speaking about all the ways of loving that have something to do with what in Greek is eros. I leave it untranslated because the spread of ideas is so broad that no one English word translates eros well. Sexual love is a common translation, but when Plato talks about eros, he makes it quite clear that eros transcends sexuality. Sexual love is only the beginnings of erosic love. Also, romance will not do because romance has a particular connotation and does not do justice to eros. Similarly with agapic love, there is no one English word that expresses the richness of the idea. Compassion is good choice. So is altruism. Yet, to use either is to miss important aspects of the other. Neither is sufficient in itself. As to your second question, yes, the order matters.

Barry: How so?

Adam: My order expresses levels of intimacy and intensity moving from the most intimate to the most universal.

Barry: I see.

Adam: Erosic love is the most intimate and intense. Most commonly in our culture erosic love is for one particular person at a time, and . . .

Lucy: [*interrupting*] Sorry to butt in. Can you clarify something for me?

Adam: Of course!

Lucy: This might sound silly, but don't we usually talk about erotic and not erosic love. I'm a little confused.

Adam: That's a good observation Lucy, not silly at all. I talk about erosic rather than erotic love because of the way erotic has narrowed in our present use. Erotic now tends to mean sexuality. In the ancient world, eros related to sexuality plus. Sexuality was only the beginning of eros. In Plato, eros ascended to the realm of the ideal where it was not sexual at all. In using erosic for love, I want to help people think beyond mere sexuality. As I was saying, this type of love is usually for just one person, and . . .

Barry: [*interrupting with a wave of his hand*] Now it's my turn to butt in! Erosic love is just for one person, you say. What, then, do you make of polyamory? By that I mean multiple, consensual, committed (that is long-term) relationships. More people are becoming open about these non-traditional erosic relationships, though they have no official sanction. There is a strong critique of monogamy.

Adam: You're right, of course. The critiques of monogamy are many and include feminist, economic, and cultural. In general, the critique is that monogamy is constructed to keep women in servitude. In other words, it is one other facet of patriarchy. There is clearly some truth to this. Patriarchy runs very deep in our culture though it is not restricted to monogamy. Polygamous cultures tend to be polygynous and allow one man may have several wives. Historically, polyandry—where a woman has more than one husband—has been less common. Patriarchy seems to be the case in contemporary Mormon polygamous marriages in the United States.

Lucy: That's certainly the case in a couple of popular TV shows about polygamy. It makes for compulsive viewing.

Adam: [*grinning*] When you should be writing an essay for my class!

Lucy: [*blushing slightly*] Of course not!

Barry: We can assume polyamory, at least on the male side. I think it would be safe to say, given the religious context, that the multiple wives do not love each other *erosically*. So, yes, patriarchy is not limited to a monogamous relationship. It's interesting that the current, and still limited, literature on polyamory is mostly by women. I won't belabor the point, but the fact of traditional, mostly religious based, polygamy and the more contemporary polyamory surely demonstrates that erosic love can be for more than one person at time.

Adam: I think it's too early to adequately assess the current social trend toward polyamory, though I suspect that true polyamory—where there is genuine and deep erosic love for more than one person at the same time— is rare. Human beings tend to be serially monogamous. Erosic love dies toward one as it grows toward another. Even where one person loves two people erosically, it seems that one of the loves is getting stronger and the other weaker. Though mammals tend not to be monogamous naturally, it is fairly clear that the human taste for monogamy is constructed as a social and cultural good. Despite its problems, we continue to hold on to it. It is deeply embedded in our culture and sense of self.

Barry: We can leave it at that, just as long as you recognize in your book that, at times, there is erosic love for more than one person.

Adam: Agreed!

Barry: Return to your four ways of loving and intimacy and intensity.

Adam: Erosic love is the most exclusive and intense. Friendship is still intense and fairly exclusive, yet we tend to have more friends than one. Affection does not lend itself to intensity. It is a more "comfortable" love. We can also have affection for a great number of people. Agapic love is the least intensive and the most inclusive.

Barry: I can see that, though it strikes me that agapic love, especially when it is compassionate, can be very intense indeed. Perhaps it is not as intense as romantic love, but it is certainly more so than either friendship or affection.

Adam: Granted. Yet, its intensity is not linked to a high level of intimacy. You hear of a natural disaster somewhere in the world and are deeply moved with compassion for these affected. It is an intense form of love. Yet, you do not have an intimacy with those affected.

Barry: That is true if you link intensity with intimacy.

Adam: My ways of ordering the ways of loving is important for another reason. I call it expanding circles of loving concern. There is movement from the one—or the few—(erosic love) to the more (friendship) to the many (affection) to the most (agapic love). As the circles expand, the intensity of love and the responsibility toward the Other becomes less. For example, my loving concern for you—as my friend—is greater than my loving concern for a stranger. My loving concern for my children is greater than my loving concern for a child who is a stranger to me.[15]

Barry: [*frowning slightly*] I agree with you. But, you know that there are many ethicists who would disagree. Take utilitarians, for example. They have argued that every human being counts equally with every other human being. Our moral obligations for our own children are no different than for children dying of starvation in sub-Saharan Africa. Each counts as one and one only.

Adam: I am aware of that. Theoretically it has some power, but in practice, I don't know anyone who could possibly live like that. Proximity counts. At the same time, I want to say that we do have loving responsibility for the stranger or the child suffering from malnutrition. But, it is not the same loving responsibility that we have for those closer to us. That is why I want to speak of expanding circles of loving concern.

Lucy: What you say sounds similar to Confucian ethics. Didn't the Master argue for the priority of family relationships over distant relationships?

Adam: Good observation, Lucy! He did. It was through learning to love those closest to us and for whom we have greatest responsibility that we learn to love those more removed. The benevolent person shows humaneness to loved-ones first.

Lucy: Others disagreed with him, if I recall correctly.

Adam: Mozi was his antagonist. He argued for the universality of love. All are to be loved equally.

Barry: And so, in ancient China we find the dispute between the particularists and the universalists.

Adam: [smiling] There's nothing new under the sun!

Scene 4

The end of the day. The two philosophers, winter coats buttoned high, almost bump into each other as they leave their respective offices.

Barry: I've been thinking about your argument. It's quite a spread of ideas! Erosic love, friendship, affection and agapic love . . . [*tumbling over his words*] Is each of these equally loving? Is any more clearly loving than the others? Can each of these ways of loving be a guide to morals?

Adam: [*with hands slightly raised in Barry's direction*] Whoa! Slow down a little. Let me try to unpack this one piece at a time.

Barry: [*smiling*] I'm sorry Adam. You *do* get me animated! Take your time.

Adam: Let me begin by saying that each of the ways of loving speaks of love, and each can properly be called love. Yet, each presents love in a different way—if you like, a facet of love.

Barry: Like the many facets of a precious stone?

Adam: Yes. For example, erosic love speaks often of passion and singularity. Agapic love is that which seeks primarily the well-being of the loved one and is often described as disinterested love. Hence, it is the kind of love most free from self-interest. Friendship is that kind of love where mutuality and reciprocation are important. Affection is the love most clearly seen between a parent and a child, or between a person and a companion animal. Each is truly love, but each shows us love in a different light.

Barry: Do you think these ways of loving can be so easily differentiated? It would seem to me that affection is often contained in friendship. Sexual attraction and friendship are not always so clearly separate.

Adam: You are right. I will make the distinctions only with the proviso that the distinctions are for analytic purposes only. The ways of loving are blurred around the edges. They bleed into each other like the washes of a watercolor painting. I don't even think we need to be tied to these specific categories, and I dare say that a different analysis would give us differing ways of loving. Yet, to think of these four ways of loving provides a useful analytical tool as we think about experiences of love. Before we talk about the ways of loving, I need to say something about appreciation. I don't think appreciation is love, but it is often that which precedes love.

Barry: Okay, by me.

Adam: Appreciation is apparent in many ways of loving. In its basic form, it is what we call "liking." To like something is not to love it, though love often begins with liking something or someone. In our everyday use of words we make a clear distinction. The young woman says to a friend about a new boyfriend, "I like him, but I don't love him." The friend knows what she means. Yet, liking is the beginning of loving in many situations. It is a continuum of feelings. When I say, "I love my new car," I am expressing a very strong liking, a strong appreciation for the vehicle. Appreciation for that which we desire is only the preliminary to love, and need not always lead to love.

Barry: So when liking becomes very strong, it is love?

Adam: That is the way we use the words in this context.

Barry: And I assume that you can love without liking?

Adam: That's true, also. Many parents deeply love their children, but there are periods in life when a parent may dislike a child! And, of course, "like" does not need to become "love." It may always be a simple appreciation. I think you can see it more clearly when we think about appreciation of the beautiful. Take, for instance, the love of a piece of music.

Barry: I'm assuming you could also say this of a great painting.

Adam: Of course!

Barry: Or any form of art.

Adam: Yes.

Barry: Come on, then! Be specific. Which piece of music? I want to hear it in my mind.

Adam: One of my favorite pieces is Edward Elgar's "Nimrod" from the *Enigma Variations*.

Barry: I love that, too! A beautiful little piece! The quiet beginning, the building to a brass crescendo, then the strings refrain—wonderful! [*pausing*] There I go using the language of love and beauty again.

Adam: [*smiling*] Our common love for that piece of music would be appreciation in a strong form. Of course, it is not reciprocal. Nimrod does not love us back. Much appreciation is like that, but is still at least preparatory to love and may be a form of love itself. As you said, "I love this piece of music." But, there is something that is very important we see with appreciation that is true of all love. Appreciation begins with strong affect. Our emotions are moved. There are feelings of pleasure and goodness.

Barry: Is love, then, just a feeling?

Adam: Not just a feeling, but also the rousing of emotion is an important part of love. I cannot conceive of love without feeling.

Barry: Nor I.

Adam: Thinking about Elgar's "Nimrod," we can also see the movement in love. If you recall our previous conversation, I suggested that love is movement from the self to the Other.

Barry: Ah, the Augustinian perspective!

Adam: The listening takes the lover (in this case, you or me) away from his own
concerns to be taken up with the Other (in this case, Elgar's "Nimrod").
When we are enamored with the Other, the positive affect—feelings of
pleasure and of goodness—leads us to connection. That is love in its
most basic form. For you or I to hear "Nimrod" is to be connected to it.
When I hear it, I do not want to stop hearing the music. I want the connection to continue.

Barry: Oddly, I have often played that piece over and again. Perhaps it is its
brevity, but it ends too soon for me!

Adam: In that simple illustration, I think my point is made. Liking something or
someone, as basic appreciation, strengthens until liking becomes love. It
would be very difficult to find a point when we switch from appreciat-
ing to loving, but the process is clear.

Barry: All very well and good. But, where is this leading us?

Adam: It's useful to show the beginnings of a relationship between love and
morality. When appreciation leads to love and love is movement toward
the Other to form a connection, that connection often leads to concern.
And concern for the Other is the beginning of a moral sense. With all
art, the appreciative lover is concerned that the art is preserved, to be
enjoyed by others, and not to be lost. It would be unthinkable for the art
to be destroyed.

Barry: There is irony here. When private collectors buy great works of art,
they often lock them away in a vault. The collector's love for the painting leads to concern for its preservation, but in secreting the picture
away, the owner saves it in one sense, but loses it to the vault. It is no
longer appreciated.

Adam: Also, collectors might just be interested in a shrewd investment with no
love for the painting at all. But, it serves to make a point.

Barry: The point being that affect leads to connection, and connection leads
to concern.

Adam: Exactly! That is both the beginning of love and the beginning of morality. I began with the inanimate because if it is true for the non-sentient,
non-personal, then it is plausible that the more personal the object of
love, the more likely that connection will turn to concern. Concern for
the Other is a fundamental moral concept. This movement of love from
self to Other is the basis of morality. I'll write about this in part two of
the book when I speak of love-itself.[16]

Barry: That will be interesting. [*pausing*] I think we had better be going.

Scene 5

The next morning, the two philosophers are walking to the Philosophy Depart-
ment from the faculty parking lot. Barry and Adam meet Molly, another philo-
sopher. Molly's interests center on feminist philosophy, sexuality, and the
ethics of care.

Barry: Hi Molly! You're just the person I was hoping we'd see today. Adam and I have been discussing his latest book on love as a guide to morals. Would you like to join the discussion?

Molly: I'd love to. What issue are you thinking about?

Adam: I've been explaining to Barry my understanding of four ways of loving: erosic love, friendship, affection and agapic love. Taken together, I think they give a full picture of what love is like in our experience. My task will be to demonstrate how love is the best guide to morals.

Molly: Sounds like a fun project. How can I help?

Barry: We've had an interesting discussion about appreciation as often the beginnings of love. Adam thinks that though appreciation need not always lead to love, it is at least the beginnings of love. When appreciation becomes strong, we think of it as love.

Adam: We were just about to chat about the way of loving I am calling erosic. I have found difficulty giving it a single meaning.

Molly: Yes, no single English word or phrase explains eros completely. What's your best shot?

Adam: I will begin with the kind of desire that is sexual attraction. Plato's initial idea is that eros is the desire for something we do not possess. At its fundamental level it is closely linked with a bodily appetite …

Molly: [*interrupting*] Like thirst or hunger …

Adam: Yes. It is a need that longs to be satisfied. Yet, sexual desire is more complex than the desire for food. A hungry person's desire for sustenance could be satisfied by any kind of food.

Molly: But, in human beings, sexual desire is often linked not just to any sexual satisfaction, but to the longing for one particular person. The desire is more than a bodily itch and is complicated by strong emotions directed toward another person. I think that is the basis for the common understanding that love and sex are not the same. To have sexual intercourse is not always to make love. Sometimes sex is just sex. Yet, sexual attraction is often the basis of love.

Adam: In our culture, when sexual desire becomes attraction for a particular Other, we call it romance.

Molly: What a mixed bag romance is! You know my view from our previous conversations . . .

Adam: Yes, Romance is relatively new in human experience and that our contemporary culture has focused far too much on it as the be-all and end-all of human experience. Romance is a product of, and supported by, consumer capitalism. Romantic myths are largely propagated by males and merely reinforce stereotypes of the woman dependent on the man.[17]

Molly: [*playfully*] You were listening! But do you agree?

Adam: [*smiling broadly*] I agree in part! In our culture, it may also be the case that males learn romance as a second language to keep females happy. Whether that relates to a socially constructed need or some biological nesting instinct, I've no idea. But I want to make sure I have heard you correctly.

Molly: You have. I lean to the idea that romance has been foisted on women by a patriarchal culture to keep women subservient. But, let's press on with your ideas. You are linking love and morality. You have your work cut out for you. I have found often that when love is mentioned, people immediately think only of romance and morality is far from their minds.

Barry: That's not surprising, as love is used presently most often in a romantic context.

Molly: A worse problem is that people assume that romance has always been a major part of human life for all people at all times and in all cultures.

Adam: And that is not true?

Molly: By no means! For instance, we assume today that marriage is based on romance. Two people fall in love and get married. The marriage is a continuation of their romance. When the romance ends (as it so often does) the marriage ends. But, historically, marriage was not about that kind of romantic idealism at all. It was about social stability, the reproduction of children and their nurturance, and economic well-being. What we now call romance was hardly a part of the picture. If it developed at all, it was after marriage and not before.

Barry: I suppose that would still be the case in those cultures where the families arrange marriages.

Molly: Exactly! Historically, you mostly find romance outside of marriage. Even in the classic tale of *Romeo and Juliet*, romance is found outside of the structures of marriage and social stability. Yet, we now expect marriage to perform the kind of role it was never intended to perform.

Adam: It's no wonder, then, that modern marriages fail as often as they do. The high romantic expectation we have placed in marriage is bound to overburden the institution.

Molly: Marriages and long-term partnerships succeed when the partners move beyond mere romance to some other kind of bond.

Adam: Like a deep affection or a friendship of the kind Aristotle called true friendship.

The three philosophers walk in silence for a while.

Barry: Molly, I too, like your analysis, but I hope you are not suggesting that we abandon romance. I'm rather fond of it myself.

Molly: No, I just think we need to reposition romance, accept it for what it is, but no more than it is. Romance needs to be cut down to size. [*after a pause*] So Adam, where do you position romance?

Adam: It is clearly a way of loving. But, like you, Molly, I think it is only one way of loving and not the most significant. Its importance lies in that when we are thinking of erosic love, it is something deeper than mere sexual attraction. It moves from physicality to personal connectedness. That is a significant shift.[18]

Barry: I think we would all admit, too, that romance at its most intense is the most powerful of all the ways of loving.

Adam: It has enormous potential as an agent for change and it has terrifying possibilities for destruction. Those gripped by eros can shift from mountaintops to valleys in seconds. Exhilarating joy can turn to the depth of despair. When "love strikes" lovers can become openhearted and generous . . .

Barry: [*interrupting*] Or utterly selfish and peevish.

Molly: So, how will you view erosic love and morality, Adam?

Adam: In two ways. First, I will suggest that it is when love is at its most intense . . .

Barry: [*interrupting again*] What we call falling deeply in love?

Adam: Yes. There is the most intense possibility of transformation. Let me give you an example. A friend of mine did not fall in love until in his mid-thirties. When he did—completely unexpectedly—his whole perspective on life changed. He documented it in a journal, which I had the privilege of reading. Life took on a whole new sweetness for him. Colors became more vivid. He was filled with compassion for others. He desired for the whole world to know the same joy that he was feeling.

Molly: But, my guess is that this did not last.

Adam: You are correct, of course. The intensity of love lasted for a few weeks.

Barry: Isn't that just infatuation and not love?

Adam: I would rather steer clear of the word infatuation. It has such a negative connotation. Haven't we been told that infatuation is something we should avoid—it's for teenagers in the flush of first-love; it's for the emotionally gullible. Yet, I want to say there is something very important about the intensity of erosic love and it is that intensity that links erosic love to morality.

Barry: In what way?

Adam: The intensity of erosic love provides a window on the possibilities of what might be. Imagine if all in the world knew the same intensity of love as my friend? The world would be changed.

Molly: And I repeat that it didn't last!

Adam: Erosic love allows us to experience possibilities for moral transformation. It allows us to glimpse what might be.

Barry: My guess would be that if what you say is true, it explains why, when the intensity fades, people often become deeply disappointed. They would rather that the intensity continues forever.

Molly: Love ruins people! Many would rather not have experienced its magnificent delights than to be let down so badly when it ends.

Adam: I agree. Yet, having tasted it, we know the possibility that such transformative love may be in our future.

Barry: But, no guarantees?

Adam: No guarantees. Which brings me to my second point about erosic love and morality. In Plato, and later in Augustine, love is a desire for something or someone we do not "have." When desire is satisfied, then love fades. In that sense, Augustine sees love as motion toward something. Love is never truly consummated. Love always remains as craving.

Barry: I recall that Plato sees sexual attraction as a rudimentary form of eros.

Adam: Yes, sexual attraction is only the beginning. In the *Symposium*, Plato has what I will call the "ladder of erosic love." The desire is first realized as craving for physical beauty and sexual satisfaction. But, it doesn't remain there. Desire for sexual satisfaction leads to other desires—for intellectual excellence and moral virtue, and, then even further to the love of goodness, truth, and beauty—the eternal realities.

Molly: So, for Plato eros has a strongly moral element in a way that we do not think of erosic love in our present usage.

Barry: That's all well and good for Plato. But I am not a Platonist. I have no room for eternal realities. Wishful thinking, if you ask me!

Adam: I accept that, Barry. I will not be suggesting that we all have to be unreconstructed Platonists to see love as a guide to morals. For the moment, my point is simply that the love we most often think of as amoral— erosic love—can be seen to have a strong link to morality. I'm sure you realize that this is the point of erosic love in Iris Murdoch's novels. She takes her cue from Plato. Eros can be powerfully transformative (and degenerative) to the way we live. I will have more to say in part two of my book when I look at the way love becomes corrupted.

Barry: Her novels are great!

Adam: Do you remember the protagonist Bradley Pearson in *The Black Prince*?[19] For much of the book, he's deeply in love with Julian Baffin, daughter of his long-time friend Arnold Baffin.

Barry: Yes, of course! Pearson's love is unreciprocated.

Adam: I will show how Murdoch suggests that romantic love, even unreciprocated, has immense power to change a life for the better, and is thus a basis for morality. At its height, erosic love is ultimately un-selfing as the lover loses himself in the beloved.

Barry: That will be interesting.

Adam: Another would be Murdoch's novel, *The Sea, the Sea*,[20] Charles Arrowby . . .

Molly: [*interrupting*] In Murdoch protagonists are typically middle-aged males of artistic disposition . . .

Adam: Yes. Arrowby retires from London's theater set to the coast where he chances upon Mary Hartley Smith, a lost love from many years before. She is now, apparently in a loveless and, perhaps violent, marriage. Hartley becomes Arrowby's obsession, even to the point of kidnapping her and forcing her to stay in his seaside cottage until she returns his love. In both stories, erosic love—perhaps the most psychologically powerful of all loves—has the potential for moral renewal. Yet, it takes an obsessive, dark turn and proves ultimately destructive.

Barry: So, two tales of unreciprocated love. I don't see much hope there was love as a guide to morals.

Adam: In both, love remains potentially a powerful moral force. The fullness of romantic love lasts for a short time. If gives a glimpse of the sheer intensity and transforming nature of love. Remember, romantic "falling in love" is only a part of erosic love. Though romance often ends in heartache (or heartbreak), equally as often romance develops into deep affection or friendship.[21]

Molly: I'm intrigued by the idea of a glimpse of the possible. Could you say just a little more about this?

Adam: [*smiling broadly*] I could give you a glimpse.

Molly: [*smiling back*] I couldn't ask for more!

Adam: The mystical traditions of religion have made much of this. Though the dominant religious perspective on love is the agapist tradition of universal, disinterested love for all, there is a minority tradition that sees the highest relationship with the divine as erosically loving.

Molly: I was hoping you would mention this somewhere in your book.

Adam: Mystics have searched for a relationship with God as the Lover and themselves as the Beloved, which mirrors the intensity of sexual love at its highest. Though in this life, the mystics enjoy this relationship only temporally, often for only brief moments, their hope is for an eternity of love with the divine.[22] Whilst many philosophers of love have suggested that agapic love—disinterested, altruistic love—is the highest form of love, there are philosophers in the Russian Orthodox tradition who see sexual love as the highest and purist form of love.[23]

Molly: A glimpse of perfect love, soon to be enjoyed forever.

Adam: Something like that.

Barry: [*ponderously*] Hmm.

Act IV

LOVE'S APPEARANCE:
FRIENDSHIP, AFFECTION, AND AGAPE

Scene 1

Sitting in the Faculty Club, a five-minute walk from the Philosophy Department across the Arts Quad. Barry brings a tray with three small cups of espresso, and a small plate of cookies. The three philosophers settle into old, overstuffed leather armchairs.

Barry: I like this place. [*looking around as if seeing it for the first time*] It's so much better than my first appointment after graduate school. No faculty club at all. This is a good place to relax and the food's not bad!

Adam: A good place for friends to be together.

Barry: Which brings us to your next way of loving: friendship.

Adam: Yes, it is the next most intimate and exclusive way of loving after erosic love.

Molly: You must be thinking of friendship in a particular way. With social networking websites such as Facebook, many people claim to have hundreds of "friends." Most of these will not be known in any intimate or exclusive way at all.

Adam: You are correct. Most of those sorts of "friends" are mere acquaintances or even strangers—acquaintances of other acquaintances.

Barry: But, surely, people who use Facebook know that many if not most of the contacts they have are not truly friends. Aren't you setting up a "straw man" here Adam?

Adam: [*taking a cookie*] Yes, I am pushing it a little. But, the fact that the designers of Facebook would call participants friends, and that people accept it, indicates that our culture generally has a low view of friendship. I will be using a long tradition of friendship that begins with the ancient Greeks, that sees friendship as a particularly strong bond between a very few people. It has a noble history and I will explain it for my readers.

Barry: I suspect many of your readers will be surprised that you include friendship as a way of loving. Many will have heard it said, or said themselves, something like, "I'm just his good friend. We are not in love." In popular understanding, friendship is distinguished from love.

Adam: You're right. That's because we have reduced love to the romantic kind and have lost much in the process. In many respects, we have impoverished love by making it so particular. Whenever love is mentioned, we assume it to mean a romantic kind. Of course, in popular usage, we do think of other kinds of love—say, in a family context, or for our animal companions—but the language of love is largely missing from friendship.

Barry: [*drinking coffee*] I tend to agree, though I have noticed in popular culture, it's becoming more common for friends to say, "Love you!" as a way of saying goodbye. It seems more common for women than men.

Adam: Yes, though men do have the "I love you, man!" for particular friends. The addition of "man" makes it clear that this is not the tender "I love you" of erosic love.

Barry: This aside, how will you convince your readers that friendship is a way of loving?

Adam: I will probably begin with a little history of the idea of friendship.

Molly: I suppose you will start with Plato, as, according to Alfred North Whitehead, all philosophy is a series of footnotes to Plato![1]

Adam: [*laughing heartily*] How could I do otherwise! [*still laughing but recovering his composure*] I will begin with the *Lysis*, Plato's account of friendship.[2]

Barry: Ah, the *Lysis*! I have always found that to be an unsatisfactory little dialogue. Little is resolved in it.

Adam: I tend to agree. It's unsatisfying that nothing is decided. But Plato does jlay the groundwork that friendship is important.

Barry: Also, that we need to be clear to distinguish eros from friendship.

Adam: That is an important point. The context of the *Lysis* is very different from ours. In the *Lysis*, Socrates holds a conversation with a number of young men, some of who are lovers and have a sexual relationship, or who want to have. There is discussion about whether friendship and sexuality can be separated. Do all friends become lovers in the sexual sense? Socrates argues not. Friendship has a higher value than mere sexual love, though a relationship that begins erosically might lead to friendship.

Molly: [*slightly frowning*] That does raise an interesting conundrum. Does friendship always lead to sex?

Adam: In our culture, we would have to give a mixed answer. We tend to assume that two men or two women could be good friends without a sexual relationship. However, we are less certain that a male and a female can be good friends without it becoming a sexual relationship. The movie *When Harry Met Sally* is based comically around the idea that if men and women become friends they will also become sexual lovers.[3] In the movie, there is an inevitability that they do. C. S. Lewis also thought that while two men could be good friends, when women and men become friends, sex would always get in the way of the friendship.[4]

Molly: I suspect this will change as our culture develops. The heterosexual norm has dictated that same-sex relationships be platonic. It has been outside the popular imagination, until recently, to transfer the "you-can't-be-friends-without-sex-getting-in-the-way" to same-sex friendships. But that is beginning to change. Perhaps we will have soon a movie, *When Harry Met Barry*, or *When Holly Met Molly!* [*giggling*] which will ask the question can two men or two women be good friends without sex getting in the way?

Adam: Socrates, of course, assumed that friendship need not lead to sex, and even if it did, friendship would outlast sex and transcend mere physicality. So, while I agree that the *Lysis* is unsatisfactory, Plato gives important hints about friendship that Aristotle later refined. Aristotle analyzes the kinds of friendship that are true and lasting and distinguishes them from temporary friendships.

Barry: Remind me of the classifications of friendship according to Aristotle.

Adam: There are friendships that are based on pleasure alone. They are often quite satisfying, but when the pleasure goes so does the friendship. Included in this type would be a friendship based on sexual pleasure.

Barry: Would that be what my students call "friends with benefits"?

Adam: I don't think so. "Friends with benefits" is about two friends who are friends for other reasons but who also provide sexual favors for each other on an ad hoc basis. If the friendship were based on the sex, then it would be more like Aristotle's second kind of friendship that is based on utility.

Barry: You mean the friends gain some mutual benefit, a kind of quid pro quo? Something for something?

Adam: Yes. Many friendships are like that. When friends are friends in some business venture, there is a clear quid pro quo. Aristotle is interested in that kind of friendship, but it is not the best kind. In fact, for the smooth running of civil society, utilitarian friendships are necessary. However, like friendships based on mutual pleasure, when the utility ends so does the friendship.

Barry: So what's left?

Adam: Friendship based on the love of the same good.

Molly: Hmm. That sounds like a difficult idea to grasp, whereas the first two types of friendship seem easy to understand. What do you think Aristotle meant?

Adam: The best friendship is when the friends do not specifically focus on each other. Instead, they focus on something external to the friendship. It is their common love for this something-other that is the basis of their friendship.

Barry: Can the something-other be anything at all? How about two friends who are friends because they share a common love for driving faster than the posted speed limit? They both love the thrill of it and encourage one another to take ever more risks. I can't see how that would be a better friendship than two businessmen who are friends because of what they can do for each other.

Adam: Aristotle counters that by saying that the best friendships are based on a mutual love for the good and not for something bad.

Molly: So what makes the mutual love of the good a better friendship?

Adam: The friendship is all the better because the two friends don't get wrapped up in each other to the exclusion of all else.

Molly: That seems sensible. I have known friends who become so entwined and focused on each other alone that the friendship became unhealthy and destructive. I can think of a number that exploded emotionally. The fall-out wasn't pretty! [*pausing to drink her espresso*] Though, it is still not easy to grasp how it works positively. Can you give me an instance?

Adam: Take two friends who come together because of their love of oil painting. They meet at the local art society when they enroll in a course titled, "Impressionism and How To Do It." After a few weeks, they gradually begin to discover that they share the same love of the good (in this case impressionistic painting). They meet for coffee after class and enjoy good discussions. Their friendship develops and they begin to share more of their social life together.

Barry: Yet, isn't there also an element of pleasure in the friendship? I can also see utility in that they use each other to critique their work.

Adam: Yes. For Aristotle that's fine. Their friendship is not based in either pleasure or utility but in the love of the good. The common love of the good will also bring pleasure and utility, but the friendship is not for the sake of these.

Molly: Thanks for clarifying that.

Barry: [*pausing while he finishes his coffee*] I think I'll have another espresso. Anyone else?

Molly: Yes, I'll have one. Adam, how about you?

Adam: Not for me Molly.

Molly: It's my turn to buy. I'll be right back.

Molly leaves for the bar. The others ponder in silence for a few minutes enjoying the ambience of the Faculty Club. Molly returns with two cups of espresso.

Barry: So is there anything else in Aristotle's view of friendship that's important for us to know?

Adam: Friends must be equals. You can't have friends who are unequal as the friendship will be one-way in some respects and not mutual.

Barry: I remember that. It was, of course, why Aristotle and many since have assumed that men and women cannot be friends. Men considered women unequal—mostly in terms of rationality.

Molly: Thank God we have left that far behind! I've friends of the kind Aristotle considered good and some of them are men. I'm including you two.

Adam: Yes I agree. But, is our friendship because we are equals? We share the same love of the good—in our case philosophy. We are all over-educated. [*smiling*] We are all university teachers. We are from the same social class. There is a great deal of equality there.

Barry: I know of a few fishermen whose commonality is their love of fishing. They all share much in common, in the way we three do. Yet, their commonality is very different from ours. Nonetheless, there is equality between them. They fit Aristotle's criteria.

Adam: The test would be whether any of the fishermen (who aren't also philosophers) could become friends with a philosopher (who isn't also a fisherman). For friendship in Aristotle's sense there would need to be the same love of the good and equality.

Molly: If the philosopher had a love of fishing, I could see a friendship developing. Though, I suspect the friendship would be centered on fishing. The
philosopher would likely leave her philosophy out of the friendship.

Barry: What if the fisherman had a love of philosophy? What if the fisherman
and the philosopher both had a love of ballet?

Adam: In a society like ours, where we have a theoretical belief in equality,
then friendship might be possible. In Aristotle's time, social role would
also be an important factor. To be a philosopher was to take a specific
role in society. For the fisherman to be considered the philosopher's
equal (and vice versa) would require one or the other to make a change
in social role.

Molly: [*frowning*] Aristotle does come over as an elitist. I doubt that he would
be as happy to call two fishermen friends in his lofty sense. Nonetheless, these ideas are worth considering. Anything else you will write
about Aristotle and friendship?

Adam: Aristotle assumes that we will have in a whole lifetime only a few
friends of the kind he describes. These are certainly not Facebook
friends. This is why, in my order of the ways of loving, I have placed
friendship next to erosic love. Deep friendships are few and far between. Not everyone has friends of the kind Aristotle advocates. Yet, it
is the friendships of this kind that make life worth living and increase
well-being. They are the icing on the cake. Of course, we can get along
quite well without this kind of friendship, but when we have it life takes
on a different quality.

Barry: Where will you take your readers next with friendship?

Adam: The obvious place is Cicero, who wrote *De Amicitia—On Friendship*.
He built on Aristotle and added his own twist. He agreed that true
friendship was rare and that it was based in virtue.[5]

Barry: What does he add?

Adam: Cicero suggests that true friends do not merely stand ready to do for the
friend what they would do for themselves, but will go further and do
more for friends than they do for themselves. Friendship should be made
carefully, cautiously, and slowly. They should not be based in politics.

Molly: Why not based in politics?

Adam: He doesn't say. That is left to our imagination!

Barry: Anything else?

Adam: Trust is the basis of friendship. When trust fails a friendship fails.

Barry: I am with you so far. I think this all makes sense about friendship, but in what sense is friendship love?

Adam: My next step in the historical timeline is helpful here.

Barry: And which time is that?

Adam: The twelfth century. Aelred of Riveaux was a monk and abbot of Riveaux in Yorkshire. He based his work on Cicero and "Christianized" it.[6]

Molly: You mean he used the same basic approach but made allusions to God in the way Christians understand God?

Adam: That's about it. But, I think his conclusions are relevant whatever your religious convictions are. For instance, he asserts that human beings are fundamentally relational.

Barry: An allusion to Aristotle again.

Adam: We have deep desires to be with other people. For Aelred, those desires are the desires of love. He suggests that the friendship love begins with desire (attraction), moves to intuition (the will inclines toward the other), and comes to fruition (an action of will for the benefit of the other). Further, friendship is beyond the kind of love we have for all people. It is more exclusive and reflects the very highest form of relationship. This mirrors the life of heaven—where all is perfect—and Aelred sees the Holy Trinity as a model of friendship. There is a lot more in Aelred, and I will explain his views in more detail in my book.

Molly: I have heard of Aelred in connection with gay love. I read that his friendship for monks in his charge was homosexual love, particularly for one young man. What would you say to that?[7]

Adam: I have read that interpretation. I think it has proved helpful for my religious gay friends to have a historical church figure whom they believe was gay. However, I am not sure we have any clear historical evidence either way about his sexual orientation. I fear, too, that to sexualize all love is a mistake.

Molly: How do you mean?

Adam: It is part of the problem I see in Freud. He reduces all of life to libido and every human action becomes sexualized.[8] For Freud, Plato's eros is simply sexuality. I believe that this is an inadequate reading of Plato.

Molly: I agree. Eros is a far more complex idea in Plato. Sex is a function of the larger human search for the perfect.[9]

Adam: It is also the reduction of love to romance that I find problematic with love as spoken of in our popular culture. If we are to broaden our understanding of love, then to reduce all love to sex is unhelpful. I suspect that part of the reason why some have difficulty making friends—men particularly—is that they are afraid their friendship will be perceived as sexual.

Barry: [*laughing nervously*] Well, then they are probably insecure in their sexuality and need to get over it!

Adam: I tend to agree. But, don't you think that in making all show of affection or tenderness overtly or potentially sexual that our culture has been impoverished.

Barry: Examples?

Adam: Take the male teacher who is now afraid to take a little girl onto his lap when she has fallen and hurt her knee for fear of being accused of sexual abuse. A male teacher comforting a little girl is often presumed to have some potential sexual misconduct afoot. Or take relationships between males and females that are assumed to end in bed. Deep friendships between men and women that are not sexual in nature are few and far between. All love has been reduced to sexuality.

Barry: What does this have to do with Aelred?

Adam: It seems to me that we are almost incapable of thinking of profound love in the way Aelred does without assuming that it must be sexual in nature. Aelred speaks in deeply loving ways about his friend. We assume it must therefore be sexual. Sexual attraction is not the deepest love. This tradition of friendship from Plato, to Aelred suggests the love of friends may be the deepest of the loves. It is unencumbered by any quid pro quo or the satisfaction of sexual desire. It is rooted in a common love of the good.

Barry: How will you relate this as a guide to morals?

Adam: [*laughing*] You don't kill your friends! At least that's a start!

Molly: Unless, perhaps, when a friend asks for assisted suicide when in extreme pain related to terminal illness.

Adam: Touché!

Barry: But, seriously, Adam. How is friendship love a guide to morals?

Adam: Two ways. First, the depth of friendship love becomes a model for what human relationships can be. It's Aelred's "glimpse of heaven." Human relationships can be this good. Second, if we are all connected to others in friendship love, then our world becomes a network of small groups of friends who all seek the good of the Other.[10] That would be a better world.

Scene 2

Toward the end of the day. In the philosophy department. Molly, with coat on and laptop case in hand, passes Adam's office. The door is open and she sees Adam and Barry in conversation again.

Molly: You two still at it?

Adam: [*grining*] We never stop. Join us if you like.

Molly: I was just on my way home. [*looking out the window to see large flakes of snow settling softly on the Arts quad*] It looks cold out there! I'll stay for just a while, but I don't want to get caught in the snow.

Adam: We were just going to chat about affection, the homeliest of all the ways of loving.

Molly: [*taking off her coat and sitting down*] You mean unattractive?

Adam: No! I'm using homeliest in the British sense, meaning simple, cozy, and comfortable.

Molly: That makes more sense! We say "homiest" on this side of the pond.

Adam: [*laughing*] I see a that, in the words of George Bernard Shaw, "a common language separates" us again. What I mean is that affection is perhaps the least passionate and intense of the ways of loving. It is perhaps the most comfortable of loves.

Barry: More like a favorite pair of old jeans or the slippers you can't bear to part with because they have become so comfortable.

Adam: When people speak of falling in love, it is not affection we say they fall into . . .

Molly: [*interrupting with laughter*] I've fallen deeply in affection with you!

Adam: Yet, affection is a very common human experience and is often accompanied by other ways of loving. Affection can lead to erosic love. It can work the other way too. Passionate, sexual love can also lead to affection. A married couple, or life partners, can have equal measures of romantic love and affection. Old friends can also have great affection for each other. Affection is also the love we most often have for animal companions.

Molly: I thought that a dog is "man's best friend," according to the old saying. So with our non-human companions aren't friendship and affection both present?

Adam: [*smiling*] That is a particular kind of friendship, but you will allow that there is often great affection in a human-canine-or-feline relationship.

Molly: Of course! Affection is a very comfortable love then.

Adam: The archetypal relationship of affection is parental affection for a child, and its complement, the child's love for the parent, though there is a difference.

Barry: I can see a clear immediate difference. Parental love is more gift-love than need-love—more focused on the child and its needs for security, safety, and affection. Parents would often forego their own needs for the sake of the child.

Adam: A child's love, at least a young child's love, does not consider the needs of the parent at all. The adult child's love takes on more of the role of affection that the parent showed to the child during its infancy.

Adam: Of course, it's quite possible that the very necessary selfishness of young children mature.

Barry: I agree. We would expect that to happen. The son who never makes the move from a childish need-love to gift-love for his mother would not have matured in his love.

Adam: As well, for the parent it is not solely gift-love. There are quite deep needs of love that are met in the parent's love for the child. Perhaps the most important work on affection and morality has been by the ethicists of care. Molly, this is your field.

Molly: Are you thinking of Nel Noddings, Sara Ruddick, and similar writers?

Adam: Yes. Though they are not explicit in speaking of affection, their work is rooted in the mother-child relationship of affection and a concomitant ethic. Wouldn't you agree?

Molly: Somewhat. I think you should root the ethics of care in Carol Gilligan's work during the 1980s. She suggested that moral language had been very much drawn from a masculine world. Moral categories were framed in ways that had been of interest to men and reflected male ways of thinking. It went so far as to suggest that the kind of morality women were concerned with was immature.[11]

Barry: Yes, that was very much the thesis of Lawrence Kohlberg, as I recall. He had suggested six stages of moral development. In his view, males were more apt to develop through the six stages than females.[12]

Molly: That was Gilligan's critique. Kohlberg had only used boys in his studies. She argued that his conclusions did not reflect girls or apply to women's concerns at all.

Adam: How did that play into the ethics of care?

Molly: From Gilligan's beginning, other feminist philosophers began to build on her work. What would ethics look like if it had been women who were the ethicists and moral philosophers and not men?

Adam: And that is how they developed the ethics of care.

Molly: Yes, care is the basic moral category, rather than justice or rationality or rules. You said before, Adam, that the basic relationship of affection is parent for child. The ethicists of care would rather say mother and child. It is that very special relationship that a mother feels for her child that is the beginning of morality. The mother is not told what she should do in the sense of giving her a rulebook. No rationality is brought to bear. She simply cares. It is the irreducible human relationship on which all else is built.

Barry: It's worth noting that mothers, who have proved unable to care, do need just such a set of rules. I don't think it detracts from your ideas Molly, but there is always an exception!

Molly: [*laughing briefly*] I can always count on you Barry to point out faults with my theories! But, seriously Adam, I think the relationality aspect of the ethics of care is quite helpful for your ideas about love. It fits in well with your people-centered rather than rules-centered approach. Nel Noddings had a useful mnemonic. She said that the ethics of care is about "receptivity, relatedness, and responsiveness." These are all aspects of the socially constructed feminine.[13]

Adam: So, Noddings argues that morality would be better built on those concerns and moral impulses that we associate with the feminine instead of the masculine?

Molly: Exactly. It would produce a morality that was more concerned with relationships than with rules.

Barry: I must add that the ethics of care is not without its critics.

Molly: Not least from among feminist philosophers.

Adam: How so?

Molly: Noddings was very careful to say that she was working on a feminine rather than a feminist morality. It was important for her that we take the feminine seriously. Historically it has been the socially constructed masculine ideas that have held the most importance.

Adam: You mean things such as strength, assertiveness, justice, a certain kind of leadership, and reasons rather than feelings?

Molly: Yes, the socially constructed feminine virtues (kindness, gentleness, care, and things like that) have not been taken seriously. The ethics of care is an assertion that those things are important for morality—at least as important if not more so than traditional masculine moralities. The critique is that by reasserting the value of those traditionally feminine qualities, Noddings has played into the hands of gender stereotypes. The fear is that the ethics of care upholds all that the old patriarchy insists on.

Barry: Patriarchy has always said that women belong in the home with children, that women are most suited to the "caring professions." I can see the potential danger in merely reasserting old stereotypes.

Adam: Yet, the importance of the ethics of care is that morality has been so lacking because it has been constructed in masculine ways. The ethics of care is a creative redressing of a balance. It is time for a construction of ethics in ways we think of as feminine. While my argument is not quite the same, I also argue for a morality rooted in notions that often have been considered feminine.

Molly: Yes, love is not a traditionally masculine idea.

Adam: I find the ethics of care very helpful for my work on love and morality, though I argue that the caring relationship is only one aspect, but a very important aspect of love.

Molly: Your work is broader than the ethics of care, then. There is not much in the ethics of care about erosic love or compassion. In fact, care ethicists are quite clear that caring is not a universal relationship.[14]

Barry: What do you mean by "universal relationship"? I can see three possibilities: a relationship that is universally present; a relationship that everyone has the ability to enter; and a universal duty to have such relationships.

Molly: The care ethicists are careful to point out that they are not arguing for a universal duty of care for all. The one-caring has responsibility only for those with whom she has a direct relationship. You can't care for everyone in the whole world.[15]

Barry: That is very different to so many ethical schemes. It is often taken for granted that we each have equal responsibility for everyone. I think that would be the point of view of utilitarians such as Peter Singer. He has argued in many books and papers that morality is about minimizing pain for everyone equally.[16]

Adam: And cosmopolitans like Kwami Anthony Appiah. He argues that there is a general duty of concern for all.[17]

Molly: The ethics of care is particular to personal relationships and not applicable universally to those with whom there is no direct relationship.

Adam: I think that is a reasonable understanding. If, as I argue, care is rooted in affection, we clearly do not have affection for all people—only for those with who we are in close relationship. However, in my analysis, care would be one of the virtues of love.

Molly: Will you explain what you mean by that?

Adam: My explanation forms the third part of my book, in which I will talk about the practice of love. For now, what interests me is that the ethics of care takes one way of loving and directly connects it with morality. I will do the same, but will connect also other ways of loving with morality.

Molly: [*standing to gaze out the window to see that the snow is falling more heavily*] I really must go. The roads worry me at this time of the year. But, I'm glad I was able to chat. Let's do it again, soon.

Adam: [*looking out the window*] I think you're wise. I'm going to leave soon.

Molly leaves the office. Adam and Barry continue their conversation.

Adam: You've given me lots of food for thought. Can we chat just a while longer about agapic love? This tradition of love is quite broad and is the usual way of loving spoken of when love and morality are linked. I am calling it the agapic tradition derived from the Greek word "agape" used in the New Testament and translated as love, though in older English, it was translated as charity (from the Latin *caritas*). It has various English names in different contexts: compassion, altruism, and Christian love.[18] But I don't want to imply that the idea is only found in Christianity. In the Buddhist tradition, for example, agape would be lovingkindness. Sir John Templeton found agape in eight major world religious traditions.[19]

Barry: How is agapic love characterized?

Adam: Often, as a love that does not seek anything in return for the lover. The lover loves the beloved irrespective of anything in the beloved that may elicit love. In that sense, it is in contrast to even the highest form of erosic love in Plato. If you recall, according to Plato, love is always for the loveliness of the object of love. For that reason, scholars such as Anders Nygren assumed that erosic love and agapic love are incompatible. Agapic love is a way of loving that treats the beloved as a subject in its own right—as an end in itself. In that sense, I think Kant's categorical imperative is a way of loving. It is also a love that can be commanded. "Love your neighbor." "Love your enemies." It is loving as an act of will.

Barry: That makes it a different way of loving compared with erosic love, friendship, or affection. I cannot imagine being commanded to fall in love! Nor to become a friend in the Aristotelian sense. Romance and friendship are gifts we receive.

Adam: Of course!

Barry: You've said a lot. Let me respond to some of your ideas. You know I am going to raise the question of whether there are any truly altruistic acts. Psychologically there is always payback. I give to a charity to help starving children and I feel good about my actions. I certainly feel compassion, but it would be untrue to say I get nothing out of my concern.

Adam: Yes, I suppose that's true. But, is it always the case? Does every act of agapic love return a feeling of well-being? Long-term care for an elderly relative—in the daily routine, without much personal reward—must come close to a pure altruism.

Barry: Quite close. Yet, I suspect others will compliment the carer and that must feel good.

Adam: To tell you the truth, I think that argument against altruism is a red herring anyway.

Barry: How so?

Adam: I don't think that genuine altruism means that there can be no return or no feeling good about altruistic actions. Altruism has more to do with intention. You see a person is some desperate need; you feel a deep sense of compassion and decide that you must do something to help. You act compassionately. Your intention is not to help so you can feel good, or look good, or have people think well of you. If that is your intention, then it is not an altruistic act. Yet, even though your act is not one calculated to give you a good return; that's what often happens. The intention is to try to help relieve the suffering of someone in need. This is most clearly love as movement from the self to the Other.

Barry: So, would you say that this kind of love is based in the need of the Other, rather than in the desire of the one loving?

Adam: Of all the ways of loving, agapic love is most clearly rooted in the Other's need—though not completely. I think you could argue that human beings are hard-wired with a deep need to help others. This is close to the idea of sentiment in David Hume. It is that which makes us human, though ethologists are also discovering something like this in other mammals.[20]

Barry: If I hear you correctly, you are saying that human beings have a fundamental need to care, but that agapic love in intention is based in the
need of the one loved.

Adam: You have heard me correctly.

Barry: Let's talk about Kant. It intrigues me that you include him in the agapic
tradition. I know that Kant found little use for romantic love. He called
it "pathological"![21] I have often wondered about the inconsistency of
the agapic tradition in that it insists that love is an imperative. "You
must love." Isn't love rather something that arises as a gift rather than
worked up as a choice?

Adam: That's true. Kant rejected love as a guide to morals because he assumed
love as desire and delight cannot be commanded—and morality in Kant
is all about imperatives to duty. Yet, his understanding of the categorical imperative is very similar to what many scholars call agapic love.

Barry: There are four formulations in Kant of the categorical imperative. Are
you thinking of any one in particular?

Adam: Mostly this formulation, "Act in such a way that you treat humanity,
whether in your own person or in the person of another, always at the
same time as an end and never simply as a means."[22] This implies respect for others and compassion for them when in need. It is the duty of
benevolence. For most thinkers in this tradition, this is a way of speaking of agapic love. So, Kant's assertion of benevolence is in the main-
stream of the agapic tradition.

Barry: I think you'll need to address this question in greater detail—whether
love is volitional or emotional.

Adam: Yes, whether love is a feeling or an act of will is a crucial question in
the philosophy of love. It has been a central element of the agapist tradition. Without a doubt, in that tradition, love is clearly a guide to morals.

Barry: In our earlier discussion, you said that you would not take a stipulative
approach to defining love. Apparently, many in the agapist tradition do
exactly that. In effect they say, "When we speak of love, we do not
mean erosic love, or love rooted in the desire of the lover, or love that
finds mutual pleasure. We mean love in a purely volitional, duty based
sense." From your Aristotelian framework, I assume that you must reject that kind of argument. In our everyday usage, erosic love is a very
real way of loving.

Adam: Yes. My suggestion, in contradistinction to the pure agapist tradition, is
to say that for love to be a guide to morals, it must include altruistic
compassion, but also affection, friendship, and eros. Each way of loving

complements the others and together they give a fuller picture of what love is. Remember, I suggest that love is one and I only make distinctions for the purpose of analysis and understanding. The ways we love meld into each other, like the beginning of dawn, when it is impossible to say whether it is still night or now morning,

Barry: So that just about brings us to the end of your consideration of the appearance of love.

Adam: In my book, that will be the end of the first part.

Barry: What remains?

Adam: If you recall my Aristotelian schema, "Life as it happens to be in our experience; life as it may become if we choose the telos of love-itself; and how to move from one to the other." I will next look at what might life be like if we move toward the telos of love-itself.

Barry: I can't wait.

Act V

LOVE-ITSELF

Scene 1

One week later. On the squash court. Barry is leaning on the wall. Adam is sitting on the floor. Both philosophers are catching their breath after a hard game. On the floor are two squash racquets and a small black ball.

Barry: You know it's after a few tough points like the ones we just played that I feel my age! On days like this, I feel like retiring.

Adam: Retiring from squash?

Barry: Of course not! Retiring from teaching. I'll play squash till I drop!

Adam: [*smiling*] That's more like it!

Barry: Are you going to the Dean's open session tomorrow?

Adam: No. I have a conflict with a student government committee meeting. To be honest, I'd rather be playing squash than either.

Barry: Me too! [*laughing*] Let's talk again about your new book. I've enjoyed your argument so far. I think you will do a good job in writing about the ways we love. But, I want to return to something that is more fundamental. I want to come back to the idea of telos. I like your idea that we can choose a purpose or goal rather than it be given to us by nature of by God. Telos is very closely related to a primary issue in ethics, which is, what constitutes our version of "the Good," or the summum bonum, as we discussed earlier. We call this a metaethical question; that is, a question that needs to be answered before we can really work on any kind of normative ethic. The question, "How should we live?" requires us to know what we think the good is. This is very difficult to answer, as supreme values, by their nature, are foundational claims. We can make such a claim but we can't prove it. We might have reasons for making the claim, but even then our claim will have degrees of plausibility or implausibility to others.[1]

Adam: Of course, I agree. And you will not be surprised when I say that I think that love is the supreme good.[2]

Barry: [*chuckling*] What else could it be! But I want to press you a little. Many have understood pleasure to be the summum bonum. Pleasure is a very natural choice for the supreme good. Non-human animals seek pleasure and avoid pain. It is a pre-rational instinctive activity. We human beings share in that. Many philosophers have suggested, therefore, that pleasure is the supreme good. It seems to fit our condition as animals. As you know, that is the basis of utilitarianism. Yet, you reject it. Why?

Adam: I am sympathetic to the position. But, I think there are other values in human relationships that cannot be boiled down to the seeking of pleasure and the avoidance of pain.

Barry: Such as?

Adam: For example, would you agree with me that truthfulness is a good?

Barry: Of course I would!

Adam: Wouldn't you also agree that, at times, to know the truth can be quite painful, or at the very least, not pleasurable? If we only consider good those things that bring us pleasure, then we exclude a large part of life. The truth may not be what we want to hear, but it is still better to know the truth than to hear a lie. The lie may bring you pleasure, but ultimately it is not helpful. In fact, sometimes things that bring us pleasure are not necessarily for our good.

Barry: An example please?

Adam: You may find that eating ice cream brings you immense pleasure. Yet, we know from nutritionists that too much ice cream is not good for us, however much pleasure eating it brings.

Barry: Of course! And that goes for many pleasurable things. So, you are suggesting that when we decide on the summum bonum, it must include something other than seeking pleasure and avoiding pain?

Adam: I am. Let me suggest acts of compassion as another example. One person cares for another for the sake of the Other and not for the pursuit of pleasure. Compassion is a way of loving. To choose love as the summum bonum is, therefore, a fuller concept than pleasure. To love can also be quite painful. Nonetheless, we love because love is good in itself, whether or not we derive pleasure from it.

Barry: I can see your point. But, I must also ask you, if you reject the hedonistic tradition, why don't you choose the eudemonic tradition developed by Aristotle? You will recall that he says the supreme good is happiness.

Adam: That's a good point. I assume you mean happiness in a different way than merely feeling happy, which can be very like pleasure.

Barry: Yes. For Aristotle, happiness was more like human flourishing.

Adam: Alasdair MacIntyre called it "being well in doing well in being well."[3]

Barry: As your argument is broadly Aristotelian, why not follow Aristotle and have eudaimonia as your pre-ethical good?

Adam: Again, I am sympathetic to the tradition. Yet, too often flourishing is seen in a purely individualistic and humanistic way. The suggestion is that you can achieve the eudemonic life on your own. In some versions, there is the suggestion that the truly happy life is where the solitary individual is self-made and needs no one else. That seems incorrect. It is counter-intuitive to that other insight of Aristotle's that we are social creatures. Well-being can only be achieved in relationship with the Other. Further, human beings are in a web of interconnections not just with other human beings, but also with non-human animals, with the earth, and with the divine. This takes the idea of eudaimonia out of the solely human into something much broader. It retains the relational understanding of life but adds other than human relationships.

Barry: You are suggesting, then, that a truly happy life can only be achieved when relationships are good.

Adam: I am, and not just between people. If you exercise cruelty to non-human animals, then your life is not one of flourishing.

Barry: If, then, relationality is included in the concept of eudaimonia, would this "modified eudaimonia" be your supreme good? [*making quotation marks with his finger in the air*]

Adam: If you mean something like well-being in relationship with the Other—the Other being human beings, non-human animals, the earth and the divine—it would. But, then I would call it love. Love-itself is the summum bonum.

Barry: [*frowning slightly*] Would it hurt your argument greatly if you dropped the divine? I hear you excluding those of us who are atheists from the good life.

Adam: For me, connection with the divine is important. However, my argument does not stand or fall on that alone. Love as the supreme good holds true even without the idea of relationship with the divine.

Barry: Very well! I'm conscious of time, but I must put something on the table for a future discussion. Even when you have chosen the summum bonum, whatever it is, it is quite a leap to say, "Therefore, we *ought* to pursue that good." For you it would be, "Because love is the supreme good, we *ought* to pursue love." I hope you will provide an argument to move us from "love is good" to "we ought to love."

Barry picks up his racquet from the floor, then stretches his back a little.

Barry: I think I've got one more game in me today.

Adam: I can manage that [tossing the ball in the air and hitting it toward the front wall].

Scene 2

After their games, Barry and Adam are walking to the locker room.

Barry: Something still puzzles me. You talk about love as if it is all "sweetness and light." You have admitted that love is often painful. Doesn't love go wrong? Hasn't love caused great human suffering? If this is true, I fail to see how love could possibly be a guide to morals.

Adam: What you say about love is true. But, I don't think we need to draw your conclusion.

Barry: Let me press this further. Clearly, not all loves are the same, and some loving relationships can be codependent, cloying, or even destructive. For love to be a suitable guide to morals, you will need to give an account of that as well. Perhaps jealousy, possessiveness, acquisitiveness, and hatred are all part of what love is. If so, that would make love a very unsuitable guide for morality. That is why even those philosophers who have looked at love and morality have excluded the erosic from being a guide to morals. In their telling, erosic love is unreliable, selfish, and often destructive.

Adam: To deal with this difficulty, I will introduce six categories: [*pausing*] "love-itself," "love-as-shadow," "love-immature," "love-corrupted," "love-misdirected," and "love-misapplied."

Barry: Are you introducing yet more ways of loving?

Adam: No. Each of these categories apply to all four ways of loving that I consider. For example, erosic love may be immature. Friendship may be corrupted. Affection may be misdirected. But to explain these more fully, I need to return to the idea of love-itself. If you recall, I will argue in my book that to imagine love-itself—the ideal of love chosen as the summum bonum, love chosen as the telos of humanity—is helpful as a guide to morals. This would be love as we might imagine it at its best, most pure and noblest. My suggestion is that love-itself in all its variety—erosic love, friendship, affection, and agapic love—is our best guide for a life of well-being and flourishing in relationship with the Other.

Barry: So, when you say "love-itself" you might say "erosic love-itself," or "friendship itself"?

Adam: Yes. We can imagine the perfect for each of the ways of loving and that is love-itself.

Barry: Yet, the loves we experience are never quite love-itself …

Adam: [*interrupting*] Exactly! Because the love we experience may be a shadow of love-itself, or immature, or corrupted, or misdirected or misapplied.

Barry: I'm listening.

Adam: Let me begin with love-as-shadow. Even our very best experiences of love are but shadows of love-itself. Erosic love, friendship, affection, and agapic love are among the most important and sought after experiences of life. That is why in many forms of entertainment—novels, movies, plays, and songs—the common theme is love. Love at its worst and its best. Love between lovers, between friends, between parents and children.

Barry: There does seem to be a deep longing in human beings for more loving relationships—particularly love that works out well. Yet, the tragedy of human life (and this too is the common theme of books, movies and songs) is that only rarely do we experience love as we would like to.

Adam: I agree. My argument is that it is that longing for love that helps us to contemplate love at its best, and that is what I call love-itself. We imagine love at its very best, with no drawbacks: erosic love without jealousy and acquisitiveness; friendship without mere utility; affection without possessiveness; agapic love without burnout. At their best, each is love-itself.

Barry: So, a kind of "pure love."

Adam: Yes, if you will.

Barry: I hear echoes of Plato. [*grimacing*] You know the kind of criticism I am going to bring, as I'm sure some of your readers will. It is Aristotle's criticism of Plato's "forms," and your analysis sounds very close to Plato. The forms were universal abstractions taken from particulars in this life, not truly part of life, as we know it at all [*holding out his racquet for effect*]. The squash racquet is a shadow of the perfect form of the squash racquet. Yet, we know the idea of the squash racquet only in a shadowy way. The true squash racquet exists in some other realm, unavailable to us. Are you arguing for this other realm with regard to love?

Adam: Not really! I find it a tantalizing notion, but it is not necessary for my argument. Rather, I am taken by the idea that we can *imagine* love-itself. Love-itself is that love than which no greater love can be imagined.

Barry: [*frowning slightly*] Now that sounds very much like Anselm of Canterbury's ontological proof for the existence of God.[4]

Adam: Yes, I will borrow from his idea and modify it.

Barry: Didn't Anselm's argument run like this: God is that than which nothing greater can be conceived. That which exists both in the imagination and in reality is greater than that which exists only in the imagination. If we can imagine something than which nothing greater can be conceived, then it must exist not only in the imagination, but also in reality, for that is greater. Therefore, God exists. Are you making the same argument to prove that love-itself exists?

Adam: No. I don't think Anselm proved the existence of God.[5] For the record, I don't think that anyone can prove the existence of God. On that point, I am with Kant. [*smiling*] But that's another story. It's not so much Anselm's proof of God's existence that interests me; it is his conception of the perfect. We can imagine a perfect love.

Barry: Now hold on a minute. I thought your argument was an Aristotelian one. You switched philosophers mid-argument. In an earlier conversation, you said you would choose love as the telos of human life. Now the notion of a telos is quite Aristotelian! Then, you begin to talk about *love as a perfect ideal*. And that sounds more like Plato. Explain yourself!

Adam: I think there is a close connection between Aristotle's "telos" and Plato's "ideal."

Barry: I'll need some convincing. For Aristotle, the telos was very much a this-world affair. Acorns and oak trees are both material, both sensual, and both empirical. Plato's ideals were in some transcendent realm, altogether unworldly. I can't see how the two notions are remotely the same.

Adam: I grant you that, but my connection is this: the telos and the ideal both signify that toward which we move. Though in one case it is material and the other immaterial, it is that which is not yet realized in both cases. When applied to humanity, the telos and the ideal both become the standard by which we measure present experience. Conceptually they differ, yet functionally they are alike. By choosing love as our telos we have that toward which to aim. By imagining love-itself—the ideal of love, perfect love, that love than which no greater love can be conceived—we see where we need to develop love. The perfect, the ideal, draws us toward something better. Iris Murdoch makes this argument for the idea of "the Good." It is sometimes called the argument from perfection.

Barry: I didn't think Murdoch was a strict Platonist. Plato believed that the ideal truly existed in some perfect realm. He did not merely imagine the ideal.

Adam: You are right. Iris Murdoch modified Plato somewhat. She was agnostic as to whether the ideal exists (as she was agnostic about whether God exists). For her, it was the fact that we can imagine the ideal that counts. The perfect draws us toward itself. In moral terms, that is the argument from perfection.

Barry: Hmm. [*rubbing his chin*] I can see the argument, but I think it is unnecessary. I am skeptical that the perfect exists. Why introduce the perfect at all?

Adam: Whether the perfect exists is beside the point. With Murdoch, I think that to imagine the perfect helps us to be become better people. Take our game of squash, for example. As we play, besides enjoying the game, we strive to become better squash players. We can imagine the perfect game of squash. It is that imagined perfect game that helps us to refine our play.

Barry: I don't think the perfect game of squash exists!

Adam: But, could you imagine the perfect game?

Barry: I will try. [*grimacing*] I suppose it would be a game where every serve was perfect. By perfect I would mean with the ball moves with the perfect weight, trajectory and closeness to the wall that the opponent could not return the serve. I would win nine straight points of perfect serves. That would be the perfect game of squash.

Adam: Well, that would be one way of imagining the perfect, but not mine.

Barry: What would be perfect for you then?

Adam: For me, the game is as much about the sociability of the activity as the perfect serve. The perfect game would be one where both players play well, are quite evenly matched, with quite a bit of drama, but where both players thoroughly enjoy the game. It would not matter to me who wins.

Barry: I disagree, but that only serves to make my point. What use is imagining the perfect when we cannot agree about what the perfect is?

Adam: When we enter the squash court, I suspect that you are striving for that perfect game that you imagined. You endeavor to make each serve as near perfect as possible. Your imagined perfect game helps you become a better squash player. It is the same for me. When I enter the court, I am looking to have a good workout, and to enjoy the to-and-fro of competition and companionship. My imagined perfect game helps me become a better squash player, too. And that is all I am saying about the argument from perfection. If we can imagine perfect love (even if our imaginings differ) we can seek to become better lovers, closer to the ideal that we have imagined.

Barry: Can't we seek to become better squash players without imagining a perfect game? Can't we become better lovers without a concept of perfect love?

Adam: Of course, we can on both counts. I am merely suggesting that to imagine love-itself, to contemplate perfect love is helpful in becoming a better lover. And, my use of the argument from perfection is only one part of my argument. Besides, when thinking about love-itself as the perfect, or the goal, I make allowances for the human condition …

Barry: [*interrupting*] You mean our fickleness, inconsistencies, and ordinary badness . . .

Adam: Yes, given that condition, we are often far from our best possible selves. And being far from our best, our loves become corrupted with jealousy, frustration, anger, power, control, and too often violence. And that brings me back to the categories of love-as-shadow, love-immature, love-corrupted, love-misdirected, and love-misapplied. Love's appearance is often in these ways. The contemplation of love-itself brings this into focus.

Barry: I'm struggling with your argument, but I will hear you out.

Adam: From what I have just said, it becomes clear that even our best experiences of love are somewhat a shadow of the perfect, of love-itself.

Barry: We are back to Plato, but I will say no more about that. Why does the knowledge that our experiences of love—even at their best—are shadowy impressions of love-itself help us?

Adam: Quite simply, the contemplation of love-itself, with the realization that the loves we experience are at best shadows of that perfection, creates within us a longing for more. And desiring more, we will pursue love above everything else.

Barry: Hmm. [*scratching his beard*] Does that not mean that we will be in a state of perpetual desire? Forever unfulfilled? And if we are always desiring and never fulfilled, then we will know the psychological pain of disappointed craving. You are giving me a recipe for suffering!

Adam: Love suffers long! [*laughing*]

Barry: I can see why the Stoics and Buddhists want us to leave desire behind. Desire is the cause of our suffering. And who wants to suffer?

Adam: I find those ideas quite appealing on one level. It would be interesting to imagine a world where there is no suffering. But, given the reality of the world—and I agree with the Buddhist wisdom that it is a world of suffering—what does love do? Love suffers with. It is because we can imagine a world without suffering, and because we see the Other suffer, that the more we love the more we suffer. To desire the perfect is to know the suffering of the imperfect. That is why love is often so very painful. Love is always shadow. Love is always unfulfilled.

Barry: Is there, then, always suffering with love?

Adam: I think so. The more you love, the more you suffer. It is our deep connectedness in love to others that means we suffer great grief when they are taken from us.

Barry: But, surely, suffering is not a good that we seek?

Adam: We do not seek suffering, but given the kind of world in which we live, we cannot escape suffering. To suffer love's loss is the flip side of knowing love's great joys. When suffering for love's sake comes our way, we embrace that suffering as a consequence of love. Those who love much also suffer much.

Barry: [*frowning*] What was your next category?

Adam: Love-immature. This is similar to shadow-love, but the emphasis is different. Sometimes our loves are simply childish—not yet grown up.

Barry: And why is that different to shadow-love?

Adam: I think it is best explained visually. In the summer of last year, I remember distinctly a beautiful July day when I found myself contemplating the basil plants growing in a pot in our herb garden.

Barry: [*longingly*] Don't make me think of summer. It can't come soon enough for me!

Adam: One plant was rather large with beautiful autumn leaves. Pretty as it was, as I contemplated, I could imagine a more perfect plant. Some of its leaves were undeveloped, some leaves had been eaten by bugs, some were diseased and black around the edges, and some were misshapen. There is no doubt it was a lovely plant, but it was not perfect. Then next to it was a small, infant plant. In many respects, it was closer to perfection that the grown plant. None of its leaves were as yet deformed, eaten, or diseased. It was lighter green in color than the older plant. Yet, it was immature. It had more growing to complete.

Barry: And you will tell me that sometimes our loves are like that?

Adam: Yes. Sometimes our love is simply immature. It is not deficient at all. It might be considered quite charming. But it needs to grow. It is love in its beginnings. As such, it is love to be nurtured, to be cared for.

Barry: Just as new-born infants are often said to be perfect. There is nothing wrong with them. They are more perfect than all the adults cooing over them. Yet, they are immature. They need loving care to grow to maturity.

Adam: You've got it! Love-immature needs to be nurtured. In that regard, it is unlike love-corrupted.

Barry: Ah, now we get to the juicy bits!

Adam: Love-corrupted is when something other than love attaches to love and makes love impure and far from love-itself. This is a particularly important category in answering your earlier question.

Barry: When I asked how love—often destructive, full of jealousy or codependent—could act as a guide to morals?

Adam: Yes. My answer is that those elements of jealousy or unkindness or possessiveness are not love at all. They are additions to love and corruptions of love. So, when we imagine love-itself, we imagine love without those corruptions.

Barry: Examples please!

Adam: Well, take possessiveness.

Barry: In an erosic love relationship?

Adam: Yes that would do. One partner who truly and deeply loves the other may become possessive, not giving the partner breathing space, wanting to know where the other is at every moment of every day. In social interactions, the partner makes it clear that, "My partner belongs to me!"

Barry: I have seen that so often! It becomes often unbearable. The love tends to get smothered.

Adam: It is clear that there is true love, yet, the love has become corrupted by something that is not itself love: in this case possessiveness. In imaging love-itself, the partner who is smothered could imagine the partner's love without the possessiveness. It would be nonetheless loving, but without the corrupting addition of possessiveness. This would also be the case with affection and the over-possessiveness of the mother who smothers her son. There is no doubt that the affection is true and deep, yet it is corrupted.

Barry: You are arguing, then, that a great deal that passes for an aspect of love is not, in fact, love at all?

Adam: Yes I am. The contemplation of love-itself helps us see that. The corruptions of love come to light before the perfection of love.

Barry: Isn't your next category love-misdirected?

Adam: It is; and it's fairly self-explanatory. There can be true love, but directed at the wrong subject.

Barry: I suppose you could really love chocolate in such a way that it is a misdirected love [*grinning*].

Adam: In that case, I've had much misdirected love in my life! [*laughing and patting his stomach*] But more seriously, let me be a little controversial.

Barry: Please do!

Adam: In our culture, one of the unchallenged agreements we have is that pedophilia is morally wrong.

Barry: You are correct.

Adam: In the agreement, there is often the unspoken assumption that the pedophile does not love the child. It can't be love because we know that pedophilia is wrong. We also know that love is not wrong. Therefore, the feelings of the adult for the child must not be love but something else.

Barry: I think that is a fair summary of the thinking in our culture about adult-child erosic love.

Adam: Here is my controversial point: it seems to me quite reasonable to suggest that the adult may truly erosically love the child. Yet, it is love-misdirected.

Barry: Misdirected because what?

Adam: It is misdirected because the child is not able to consent to sexual acts and is still too immature to make autonomous decisions. Also, there is an abuse of power relationships. [*pausing*] Love is also misdirected when love is directed at bad objects or for bad ends.

Barry: I gather here again it may truly be love?

Adam: Yes, but love for something that causes harm …

Barry: [*interrupting*] Like love of violence?

Adam: Or love that works toward a bad goal.

Barry: Sounds like the Bonnie and Clyde syndrome. Two lovers whose love is directed at criminality.

Adam: [*smiling*] My final category is love-misapplied. Here my suggestion is that the word "love" is applied to something that is not love.

Barry: Didn't you mention this when we spoke of self-love?

Adam: Yes I did. Sometimes, we say something is love when it is not at all. "I love you," may mean I am grateful for what you have done. "Love you!" when used at a parting may really mean, "Bye for now!" "I love my iPhone" may mean, "I like this piece of technology. It is quite useful to me. I am glad I have it." To call any of this love is to misapply the word.

Barry: Are you saying that, in our culture nowadays, we use the word "love" a little too freely?

Adam: Yes. By our overusing the word "love," we have cheapened what love is. For love to be a guide to morals, we need to clearly identify when love is misapplied.

Barry: Here, I do agree with you.

Adam: All in all, this is how I will deal in my book with your accusation that I only see love as "all sweetness and light."

Barry: It wasn't really an accusation—merely an observation.

Scene 3

Later that day in the Faculty Club. Barry and Adam have just finished a meal. On the table a half empty bottle of wine, two glasses and two small plates with the remains of cheese and crackers.

Adam: Don't you think the new chef is a great improvement on the last one? The food has moved from unbearable to very enjoyable. What a difference!

Barry: I completely agree. I've eaten far too much. I think we need to sit a while and let it digest. [*leaning back in his chair and unbuttoning the top button of his trousers.*] Let's get back to your book. I am intrigued to know how you are going to make the leap from love as we know it to a moral claim that we should be more loving. My problem with much that you have said so far is that you have not yet said anything about the "is/ought" question. Hume proved conclusively for me that you simply cannot say what *ought* to be the case from what *is* the case. Logically, a prescriptive conclusion—and ethical conclusions are always prescriptive—can only result from prescriptive premises. What is the case is always descriptive and descriptive premises will never give a prescriptive conclusion.[6]

Adam: Yes, that's the way logic deals with ethical arguments.

Barry: To reach an ethical conclusion, there is always a value statement in the argument, though often hidden, which determines the moral ought. An example I have often used with students is this little argument: "It's very cold outside, therefore you ought to wear gloves." We use these kinds of argument all the time without realizing that something is hidden. The fact that it is very cold does not necessitate the "ought" of wearing gloves. The argument really is this: "It's very cold outside. If you go outside without gloves, your hands will freeze. It is a bad thing to allow your hands to freeze. Therefore, you ought to wear gloves." The prescriptive premise is: "It is a bad thing to allow your hands to freeze."

Adam: It's even more complex. The argument could be expanded to explain why it is bad to let hands freeze. Freezing hands cause great pain. Pain is universally considered something to avoid. The hidden prescriptive premise is: Pain should be avoided.

Barry: Let's apply this to your argument about love. Your conclusion is something like, "We ought to be more loving," or "We ought to pursue loving ends," or "We have a duty to love." So far, your argument is this: "These are the ways of loving we experience in everyday life, erosic love, friendship, affection and agapic love." How will you move from those descriptive premises to your prescriptive conclusion?

Adam: I grant you this is difficult! The trajectory in moral thinking after Hume, at least followed by G. E. Moore, was to find the prescriptive by intuition. We cannot prove in any scientific or empirical way what we ought to do, so we simply intuit it. Intuitionism suggests that, in ethics and aesthetics, we cannot make a reasoned argument. We simply intuit what is good or what is beautiful. Moore had reached the conclusion that there could be no reasonable justification for the concept of "good." Good, like "yellow" is a foundational idea that cannot be divided into parts, and is not derived from anything else. It just is. How do we know the good? According to Moore, we know it by intuition. For Moore, intuition dictated that friendship and contemplating the Good are a guide to morals.

Barry: How would it be if you used Moore's argument?

Adam: It would be to say that we intuit simply that love is good and that we should seek to be more loving. If you ask why, the answer would be, "Because it is so!"

Barry: For those who came after Moore, particularly the logical positivists, intuitive statements, in fact all moral statements, were not in any sense truth claims. They were merely expressions of preference. They abandoned moral language as making any sense. Those philosophers tended

to agree with Moore's analysis and agreed that we cannot reasonably jus-
tify a moral value like "good." However, they rejected his intuitionism. It
left them with the conclusion that moral claims were not saying anything
at all other than the expression of personal preference. In my view, they
correctly exposed Moore to be saying nothing more than, "It feels right
to me." So, if you argue for, say, generally increasing pleasure as a basis
for ethics, all you are saying is that you choose to value pleasure more
than something else. It may have no further meaning than that.[7]

Adam: So you agree with them against Moore?

Barry: I find Moore appealing in his own way, but his theory does not stand up
to the rigors of an analytical argument. There are massive holes in his
argument. It's no wonder his views very soon fell out of fashion.

Adam: I'm not so ready to consign intuitionism to the trashcan of history. Ethical intuitionism has been made a caricature and somewhat misrepre-
sented. In all likelihood we are all closet intuitionists.

Barry: How do you figure that?

Adam: Well, an intuition is a belief that is not based on any other belief, not is it
justified by any line of reasoning. It is a bottom line claim to knowledge. An intuition is pretty close to the notion of prima facie moral
axioms, or basic ethical beliefs. We discussed this some time ago when
we talked about the practice of love looking very like basic ethical beliefs.[8] That we should do no harm, or that we should do to others what
we would like them to do to us needs no justification. Also significant is
that these same moral ideas are intuited in all cultures that take moral issues seriously. [*pausing*] Yet, Moore's legacy opened the way not only
for logical positivism, but also for ethical relativism—any particular
ethical claim is equal to any other.

Barry: And relativism is quite a winsome argument—at least if you listen to
first year philosophy students!

Adam: Who listens to first year philosophy students?! [*laughing*] Relativism
has also been very strongly criticized and is not ultimately convincing.[9]

Barry: Will you explain their ideas in your book?

Adam: I shall.

Barry: Let me recap. Hume made an important claim: that we can't derive moral ideas (ought) from descriptive facts (is). We need to find our "ought"
somewhere else. Moore suggested intuitionism. Philosophers, after
Moore, found his intuitionism wanting, and philosophically we were

left with relativism. It would seem the answer, then, is to do what feels right to you, or not. This isn't a very hopeful moral situation!

Adam: Agreed! But it is not the only trajectory after Hume. Not all philosophers think that Hume's is/ought dilemma is correctly framed. In many respects, it was the beginning of the fact/value dichotomy and there has been useful critique of that.

Barry: After Hume, a clear distinction was made between facts, which are scientific and empirically provable and values that are mere expressions of preference.

Adam: The distinction is not as clear as some have thought. As the pragmatists have said, "knowledge of facts presupposes knowledge of values."[10] Yet, despite this, I am still convinced that, in moral argument, Hume is correct. We cannot derive moral conclusions from merely descriptive premises. What we need is careful thought about the way we derive our values. How do we form prescriptions? How is a moral sense developed?

Barry: You are full of good questions! But do you have any answers?

Adam: In my book, I will suggest three interconnected ideas. I call them the affective, the reflective, and the elective components to moral sensibility. I will explain how each component builds moral sense, and then I will apply it to love as a guide to morals. I begin with Hume, for he gives us the first clue about moral sensibility. I make a different trajectory after Hume and Moore than that taken by the logical positivists.

Barry: I'm intrigued.

Adam: During and after the eighteenth-century Enlightenment in the Western world, philosophers struggled with how we make moral sense of life. Before the Enlightenment, it was the case that, for most people, religion answered the question. There were different religious answers, but, by and large, if you were Catholic, you would look to the Church and its centuries of developing tradition. If you were Protestant, you would be more likely to say that the Bible held the clue to making moral sense of life.

Barry: [*interrupting*] Was there no alternative?

Adam: Judaism was a minority tradition, but it, too, looked to its developed religious ideas to make moral sense of life. To be irreligious was not really an option. During the Enlightenment, religions began to be questioned as a guide to morals and philosophers suggested three ways we make moral sense of life. In broad terms, the philosopher associated with morality rooted in thoughtful reflection was Kant. He argued that reason would tell us what our moral obligations are. David Hume argued differently. For him, it was the feeling of sympathy (with benevolence) where morality was rooted. He famously said that reason was only ever and ought only ever to be a slave of the passions.[11]

Barry: [*laughing*] And hasn't that caused some controversy over the years! It's not totally clear what he meant by that, but it certainly made room for feeling alongside reason. For most of moral history, the passions were deeply suspected. The passions are like wild horses that need to be tamed. You find that tradition in both West and East.[12]

Adam: Søren Kierkegaard suggested morality should be guided by radical choice. Morality is not merely reasoning or feeling but authentic choice. It was the human ability to choose that made human beings moral animals. In some respects, this was a development of Kant who saw morality rooted in reason, but directed by a "good will."

Barry: Yes, that is why some have claimed that Kant was the father of existentialism. His emphasis on the will resonates with later existentialists. [*pausing*] So, which of the three are you going to argue for?

Adam: [*grinning broadly*] All of them together! I will say that we develop a moral sense at the intersection of all three. I am quite taken by Hume's suggestion that the morality begins with our feelings. We encounter life in all its variety, complexity, and difficulties and we feel a certain way about it. With Hume, it strikes me that the moral feeling is the feeling for the Other. It is the human feeling of empathy with the plight of the Other—the ability to put us in the shoes of the Other. Their situation could well be our situation. We share sorrows and joys. We know to some degree how the Other feels because we too have felt in similar ways. Yet, feeling alone is not the completion of moral sense. Reason comes to feelings aid. This is how I feel, but what do I think about how I feel? Why do I feel this way? Since I feel this way, is there any obligation on my part toward the Other. Is action required to bring about some change on behalf of the Other? This is where choice enters the moral picture. I may have certain feelings; I may reason that my feelings require some kind of moral response. However, if I choose not to act on my feelings and thoughtful reflections, moral sense is not completed.

Barry: Can you give me an example of how this works practically?

Adam: I can give you an example from the classroom. As you know, most of my classes relate to moral philosophy. Part of my task is to help students think through a moral philosophy for themselves. Yet, I am aware that students make the most progress when the class is not a mere exercise in reasoning. Students need to be aware of how they feel and why they feel a certain way. They also need to develop the skills necessary to listen to their feelings, to reflect on them and to be able to make authentic choices.

Barry: How do you help them to feel?

Adam: I use a variety of techniques that I'm sure you use as well. Among them are film (documentaries and dramas), stories, music, memories of events in the students' lives, and events in the media.

Barry: I see. So, you elicit feelings and then have the students reflect on what they feel and why they feel it. I do the same, though I have not consciously thought of it in the terms we are speaking of now.

Adam: The development of moral sense requires the insights of all three of the great Enlightenment philosophers, the combination of the affective, reflective, and the elective. Love begins in feelings about the Other, but is aided by reflection on those feelings, and love requires choices. Think about the young woman who falls in love with her friend. It is clear that love begins in the emotions. She does not first choose to love her friend, nor does she think about loving her friend. She feels love. But then, she reflects on her feelings. She weighs the consequences of her love. She thinks through the impact of her love on others with who she is in a relationship. She thinks about the cost of her love. There are many considerations, and much to be considered. And then she makes choices: whether to continue the relationship or to break it off, when to see her new lover, whether and when their love should be physically sexual. It is a further reason why I suggest love as a guide to morals: moral sense and love both share the intersection of feeling, thought and choice.

Barry: Can you say more about Hume. I'm intrigued. He is not always easy to interpret, but I understand Hume's position to be that morality derives from the natural inclination we human beings have toward sympathy and benevolence. These seem to Hume to be so much part of the human picture that morality is a form of naturalism. I have always found the conception of nature problematic. Often, what we claim to be "natural" is none other than the sensibilities of our particular time and place. Hume was very much the eighteenth-century enlightened gentleman. His sympathy and benevolence, though they seemed natural so him, were the socially constructed mores of his day. Hume's naturalism is an issue for me.

Adam: I tend to agree. But, what I find very appealing is his understanding that affections are the root of moral sense. In other words, we feel things. And our feelings are often strong enough to lead us to an "ought" or a "should." Whether those feelings are entirely natural, as Hume suggests, or whether through family socialization, or through long tradition and enculturation they are embedded in society, matter little.

Barry: So, the point you are taking from Hume is that feelings are a large part of moral sense?

Adam: Yes.

Barry: Doesn't that somewhat go against the grain of much moralizing. I'm thinking of the "feelings are untrustworthy, go with reason" and "the passions need to be controlled by reason" styles of argument.

Adam: You are correct again. Yet, there has been a minority moral tradition that has focused more on sympathy. That would certainly be my reading of the Buddhist tradition. It would also be the morality of love espoused by the early Christian church before the fourth century and the acceptance of Christianity by declining Rome.

Barry: Ah, Christianity's slide into becoming the religion of empire!

Adam takes a cracker, adds cheese, and eats for a while.

Adam: [*licking the crumbs from his right thumb and forefinger*] Of course . . . [*licking his fingers again*] the reflective is also important in determining moral sense. In other words, we get our values by thinking about them.

Barry: That sounds like Kant to me. Wasn't his view that reason will guide us in moral matters? You surely know the problems with that view?

Adam: Kant assuming that reason is universal and reason in any culture, any age, and by any person would result in the same moral prescriptions.

Barry: That is so problematic! Ways of thinking are very culture-bound. What seemed obvious to Kant in eighteenth-century Prussia might not seem so obvious to someone in the ancient world, and not so obvious to folks in cultures other than his own. It assumes that only one way of reasoning exists. In Kant's version, it is the rationality of the educated, eighteenth-century, male elite. There are many ways to think. The appeal to reason can be a thinly veiled endorsement of the status quo.

Adam: I agree if taken on its own. But, I want to take both Hume and Kant seriously, and take them together. They both say something significant. Hume helps us see that our values arise in the first instance from our feelings. But feelings alone are insufficient for a sustained moral understanding. It is important for us to know why we feel the way we do. To use Hume's metaphor, reason as a servant comes to passion's assistance.

Barry: I am longing for an example to make this clear.

Adam: Take cruelty, then. When we see a cruel event, most of us respond viscerally. It is a deep feeling of revulsion toward the action. It is a deep feeling of empathy with the victim of cruelty.

Barry: Example, please!

Adam: I was out walking in a park some years ago, along a gently flowing river. There was a little boy apparently playing with something by the bank. I ambled along to take a look. To my horror, the little boy had captured some young frogs and was systematically pulling off their front legs. It was clear that the frogs were distressed, but he simple laughed at them and wanted to see how frogs managed with only back legs.

Barry: How revolting!

Adam: You asked for it! It was a clear case of cruelty. When I saw it, I felt as you just did. What we see matters to us, and we know it matters because we feel very strongly. Needless to say, I gave the little boy a talking to about cruelty!

Barry: Good for you!

Adam: But, it did raise the questions: Why did I feel like that? What made this action a cruel action? Why was it a moral issue? Why is cruelty wrong?

Barry: I see. And the answer to those questions does not come from the feelings, but from thinking about why you felt that way; why the lives of the little frogs mattered to you; and why you felt you had a responsibility to help educate the boy.

Adam: And the reasons I came up with were reasons like causing unnecessary pain, victimizing a helpless Other, respect for all things in nature, the dehumanizing nature of cruel actions to the one performing the cruelty, and a host of others.

Barry: I see your point. How we should live is a particular kind of question. Its basis is an understanding of worth or value. In this respect ethics is like its philosophical twin aesthetics and an understanding of beauty. Aesthetics and ethics are based on what people value in any particular culture and time. You are suggesting that what we value is shown to us first by what we feel, and then by how we think about what we feel.

Adam: Yes, but before I say more about reason, there is another way of thinking about morality that I will mention in my book. That is to suggest that morality is deeply ingrained in human nature. Human beings are moral beings and if we look carefully enough, then we will discover morality. In my terms, it would be to say that the sentiment of love is so deeply ingrained in the human psyche that it would seem reasonable to argue that we should work with the grain.

Barry: That sounds like an argument from Daoism. The *Dao*—the Way—is understood to be the grain of the universe. The human task is to find the *Dao* and to align with it.[13]

Adam: Yes, Daoism is one of its Eastern formulations. In the West, it has more often been termed the natural law tradition. It began with Aristotle and found a vibrant expression in Aquinas, who added the concept of God to Aristotle's naturalism. Nature tells us what is good. Or for Aquinas, nature, created by God, tells us what is good.

Barry: It's a little esoteric for my taste. I prefer a more logical argument. In practice, it reminds me of Moore's argument from intuition. In Kant, reason guides us; in Chinese philosophy, it is the *Dao*; in natural law, it is nature; and in Moore, it is a built-in intuition. Though there are clearly differences, it seems they are all making an argument for something similar.

Adam: Yes. I want to say a little more about reason, and particularly Kant's understanding of how it helps form moral sense. Kant spoke of the categorical imperative. This is a moral ought that is derived form reason and is applicable at all times, in every situation and across all cultures. It is a categorical imperative because the morality commanded is a good in itself and is not a means to some other good. He had several ways of speaking about the categorical imperative. This is one of the most important: "Always treat the person, in yourself or another, never merely as a means to an end, but also as an end in themselves." So, for Kant, human beings are a good in themselves. They are not to be used as a means to some other good.

Barry: That has been a very important way of thinking about morality. It underlies much of the moral theory we call rights. That are some rights that belong to people simply because they are human beings. I think respect is now one of the more important moral ideas in our culture.

Adam: Yes Kant's ideas have been very influential, even if we can find problems with his thinking as a whole. I do not take his approach to categorical imperatives, and I don't think that reason alone would lead us to them.

Barry: Nor do I.

Adam: I am more taken by Kant's idea of the hypothetical imperative.

Barry: The idea that a moral ought is not self-evidently true and discovered by reason, but rather based on some condition.

Adam: Yes. Kant did not consider hypothetical imperatives truly moral claims at all. For him, a moral claim could only be established by pure reason. The hypothetical imperative is something you ought to do if you want to achieve a certain end.

Barry: So, if you want to become a good squash player, you ought to practice. The practice is not an end in itself, it is a means to become a better squash player.

Adam: [*beginning to pile the dirty plates*] I call hypothetical imperatives "if-then-should" moral axioms. The "should" is dependent on being able to define the "if." This is more helpful to me. Even Kant's categorical imperatives seem to me to be hypothetical. We treat people with respect and as ends in themselves, if [*emphasizing word*] we have already determined that human beings are ends-in-themselves. We should tell the truth, if [*emphasizing word*] we have determined that the only way society can function is when there is a base of truthfulness. Here reason is involved in determining first what the "if" is, and then in deciding what we should do in order to fulfill the if. All Kant's categorical imperatives seem to collapse into hypothetical imperatives. So, it seems to me that all moral claims are of the nature, if-then-should.

Barry: The key, then, is to decide on the if; what the condition is that is to be fulfilled. For you, Adam, the if, though I hardly need say it, must be to maximize love.

Adam: [*sweeping crumbs from the table into his hand and wiping hands together letting the crumbs fall on the empty plate*] If we want to know well-being in relationship with the Other, to live a life of love—for love is the telos of life—then certain things follow. Reason comes to our aid in helping us work out what these things that follow are. Yet, even then, moral sense is not complete without the third component. I call this the "elective" and it refers to choosing to do the moral action that feeling and reason have led us to. This would be the argument from radical choice that Kierkegaard makes. In his *Works of Love*, he argues that love as a guide to morals is based on the existential radical choice to love.[14]

Barry: Yes, in *Either/Or*, Kierkegaard makes an argument for personal decision making and responsibility—radical choice.[15]

Adam: And radical choice is based on critical reflection, which is in part my argument. But, the point I want to make is Kierkegaard's emphasis on taking an active role in shaping who we are in process of becoming. It is not merely feeling, nor merely thinking, but commitment to the ethical life that is equally important.

Barry: It is interesting to see that the three arguments for love as a guide to morals cover the reflective, the affective, and the elective aspects of the human psyche.

Adam: Yes. Kant bases morals in reason, Hume in feelings, and Kierkegaard in choices. Though of the three, only Kierkegaard sees love as a guide to morals. However, I think both a Kantian kind of argument and a Humean kind of argument can also be used to support love as to guide morals. [*pausing*] But, it is radical choice that makes the bridge between love's appearance, love-itself and love's practice. To move from reflection to practice requires the kind of commitment that Kierkegaard speaks of. The ethical life does not merely happen. It requires resolve: the radical choice of will to practice a certain way, to take control of one's life.

Barry: A subject for another day, perhaps. Let's go home!

Act VI

LOVE'S PRACTICE

Scene 1

Four weeks later. Adam and Barry are walking to the university sports' center.

Barry: Adam, it's been a while since we talked about your book. I hope it's coming along well.

Adam: Not as well as I'd hoped. I have a mountain of grading interfering with my writing. But, I'll get back to it in the next week or so.

Barry: If I recall correctly, you are making a form of Aristotelian argument. It runs something like this: first, untutored human-nature-as-it-happens-to-be; second, human-nature-as-it-could-be-if-it-realized-its telos; and finally, practical ethics as means to transition from the first to the second. Further, you have modified Aristotle to suggest that there is no natural telos available to human beings. You suggest rather an elective telos: a goal that we can choose. The telos you choose is love. You also suggest a way to dodge Hume's is/ought problem by resorting to a threefold moral sense involving feeling, thinking and choosing.

Adam: That's a good summary. So far, we have talked about the loves we experience in our everyday life. I call the first part of my book, "love's appearance." Then we considered what life might be like if we realized the telos of love. That part I called, "love-itself."

Barry: And the third part of your book will look at the argument of how we might move from one to the other. Remind me, what will you call that section?

Adam: "Love's practice."

Barry: Ah, yes! Now I remember. Can you explain more fully this part of your book.

Adam: With pleasure! I will need to talk a little more about Alasdair MacIntyre's ideas. He suggested, after Aristotle, that a moral life is not so much about rules and why we ought to follow them, but rather, about the kinds of people we should become.

Barry: Virtue theory, we call it.

Adam: MacIntyre explains the virtues that make up character—the kind of people we are—in terms of a practice. A practice is a complex form of human activity through which the good internal to the practice is reached.[1] The good of a practice is that toward which the practice aims.

Barry: In other words, the telos.

Adam: Yes. And a practice is part of a tradition. It is the tradition that gives the practice its telos. Further, a practice has a set of virtues associated with it. It is through acquiring the virtues of a practice that the telos of the practice is achieved.

Barry: And how does one acquire the virtues of a practice?

Adam: Through the building of daily habit.

Barry: It seems we have: a tradition, that suggests a telos, that requires a practice, that is made up of virtues that are achieved through daily habit, that realize the telos.

Adam: That's about it.

Barry: This is a complex set of ideas. As always, can you give me something more concrete?

Adam: We could take the game of football.

Barry: [*grinning*] Do you mean American football or soccer?

Adam: [*also grinning*] I mean soccer—the beautiful game! There is a long tradition of football playing that dates back to the nineteenth century. As the tradition developed, it became increasingly clear that the purpose of football was for two teams to play against each other, kicking a circular ball into a space called a goal. This became the practice of football. It is a complex social activity with a telos internal to the activity. But to engage in the practice—to achieve the telos—requires certain virtues related to how to kick a ball, passing, shooting, how to head the ball, how to play by the rules, how to develop teamwork, and so on and so on. All of those virtues are learned through the building of habit that requires day-by-day skill-building in each of those footballing virtues. When the virtues are learned and become "second nature," the good internal to the practice of football is achieved.

Barry: I follow you so far. How will you apply this to the moral life?

Adam: It takes us back to the question of the good of a human life. Following MacIntyre, I suggest that the good toward which we aim—the telos—is provided by a long tradition of moral thinking. To achieve that good requires a particular practice of human living with its associated virtues.

As we develop those virtues, we move toward the telos. A long tradition suggests that love is the telos of human life. So, a loving life is one that has achieved the good of human life. The practice of a loving life will require the virtues of love. The virtues of love are developed by the daily habit of acquiring them. In this way, love is a guide to morals.

Barry: By making love the telos, you can speak of love's virtues in the plural. Is there any sense in thinking that love itself is a virtue?

Adam: Yes, I think there is. As love is one, so love's virtue is one. However, for analysis I will speak of the twelve virtues of love. There are probably more, but twelve is as good a number as any, and the twelve I will suggest have coherence.

Barry: And they are?

Adam: Goodness, no-harm, courage, fairness, kindness with gentleness, care, faithfulness, reparation with forgiveness, respect with attentiveness, non-possessiveness, moderation, and thankfulness.

Barry: That's an interesting list. I will make an immediate comment. Of the four classic virtues, I hear courage, moderation, and justice (if that is what you mean by fairness), but surprisingly I don't hear wisdom. [*raising his eyebrows*] Where is wisdom?

Adam: I have omitted wisdom for the simple reason that love-itself is wisdom.

Barry: How so?

Adam: The English word philosophy, as you know, comes from two Greek words: love (*philia*) and wisdom (*sophia*). Philosophy is often said to be "the love of wisdom." However, as French philosopher Emmanuel Levinas suggests—and Luce Irigary, another French philosopher, agrees with him—philosophy is "the wisdom of love." Just as theology is the discourse about God, and metrology is the study of measure, and zoophilia is the love of non-human animals, so philosophy can be said to be the wisdom of love. To live a life of love is to live a wise life. Love is itself wisdom.[2] To put it another way, the twelve virtues of love form the wisdom of love. Love's wisdom is contained in the virtues of love's practice.

Barry: Of course, for the ancient Greeks, the word we translate as wisdom was not *sophia* (wisdom in the general sense) when listed as one of the four cardinal virtues, but rather *phronesis* (practical wisdom). They made a distinction between wisdom as the search for and knowledge of universal principles and practical, everyday wisdom. That's why it is often translated as "prudence." *Phronesis* was a very important idea for Aristotle.

Adam: Indeed it was! My argument is that love is both wisdom in the more general sense (*sophia*), and wisdom as practical application. That is, the best way to act in any situation is always the way love dictates. So, if a given situation requires goodness to be exercised, that is *phronesis*. If a situation needs forgiveness to be present, that is *phronesis*. If a situation needs kindness, that is *phronesis*. For that reason, I have not included wisdom as one of the virtues of love—love-itself is wisdom.

Barry: I would like to hear you say more about each of these virtues of love.

Adam: Before I do, I want to make something else clear. Each virtue has a corresponding habit. The virtue is a state and the habit is an action. Take kindness, for example. Kindness includes the action of being kind toward the Other (doing kind actions, a habit), and becoming a kind person. The two are intimately connected. Repeated kind actions will tend toward a more permanent state of kindness. To be in a state of kindness (being a kind person) will tend toward the carrying out of kind actions.

Barry: You say this is true of all virtues. So we can say that a virtue contains both noun and verb forms, and that the verb form is a habit?

Adam: Yes, though in English, for some virtues, we need to add another verb. Love is both a noun and a verb—"love" and "to love." Gentleness is a noun but its verb form would be, for example, "to show gentleness."

Barry: I suppose it also becomes an adverb—"to act gently," and even an adjective "a gentle touch."

Adam: Yes. Noun and adjective, verb and adverb, show that virtue is both state and action. [*pausing*] So, let me begin with my list of love's virtues. My first is goodness. I was tempted to call it "beneficence," but that word is not one we use frequently in everyday speech. Its meaning—to seek good for the Other—is the primary virtue of love.

Barry: And now we're back to that "old chestnut" of philosophy, namely, "What is good?"

Adam: I can only answer as I have before, that I modify Aristotle's conception of human flourishing as the good by adding that it is flourishing in relationship with the Other. The good is never merely an individualistic idea. The virtue of goodness is to develop the habit of always seeking the best for the Other. If I love you, then I will always seek your good. I will want you to flourish.

Barry: To say such is a little nebulous isn't it? How do you know what it is to flourish? What if the lover acts in such a way believing that the Other will flourish, and in fact the opposite occurs?

Adam: [*frowning slightly*] That is a difficulty. The consequences of an action, produced from loving intention, may not always promote the flourishing of the Other. That is the risk of love. Love is in the intention that produces the action.

Barry: Can you unpack that a little more?

Adam: A loving intention to seek the good of the Other will always consider potential consequences. The consequences of an action have a direct bearing on the good of the Other. Yet, consequences are often far from certain. It is for that reason that intention is so important in moral choices. The lover intends good for the Other. Consequences will be considered, but, at the moment of choice, risk is taken. It is an existential moment of genuine choice.

Barry: This sounds like Kierkegaard's "leap to faith."

Adam: Yes, to love is to take such a leap. It is always risky, but love is always worth the risk.

Barry: If you'll allow me, I'd to ask a practical question: how would you prepare to take such risks?

Adam: This is where habit comes in. For Aristotle, virtue is created by small acts of virtue. To become a courageous person requires that you learn the daily habits of taking small courageous actions. In time, courage becomes a part of the person you are—a part of your make up. Then, when a great act of courage is required you are able to take it because you have developed the virtue of courage. You have become a courageous person. Little acts of goodness on a daily basis, seeking the good for the Other in each situation, develops the virtue of goodness. As goodness is one of love's virtues, you become in time a more loving person.

Barry: This would apply to all the virtues you name?

Adam: Yes. Shall I carry on with my explanation of love's virtues?

Barry: By all means!

Adam: I continue with no-harm.

Barry: As you rejected beneficence as a word not in general use, I assume you also rejected "nonmaleficence," for the same reason.

Adam: Yes I did. But, I have toyed with using the Sanskrit word *ahimsa*, which Gandhi used often. It literally means the avoidance of violence.

Barry: Is the avoidance of violence, as an aspect of love, significant for you?

Adam: Yes. I will argue that love-itself is always nonviolent,[3] that love causes no harm to the loved-one. To do no harm and to do good form an indissoluble pair.

Barry: In what way?

Adam: Some argue that sometimes to do good may require the use of violence. This is the argument sometimes known for short as the "ticking time-bomb."

Barry: Ah yes! In its current form it goes like this: A suspected terrorist is apprehended. To prevent a greater act of violence, the terrorist is tortured. Violence is used against the one for the sake of the well-being of the many. That is a fairly standard defense of the use of violence.

Adam: It is the argument used for fire-bombing Japan in spring 1945, and then for the use of atomic bombs in the summer of the same year. Toward the end of the Second World War, many U.S. and Japanese soldiers were locked in terrible conflict in the pacific Islands. To do good toward the U.S. soldiers on the islands meant using extreme violence against Japanese cities, killing thousands of civilians. The destruction of the cities prompted the early end of the war, and so the saving of thousands of American servicemen. So the argument goes.

Barry: I can see the logic of that position. The greater good, at times, demands violence. I will push you on this a little. In one of our earlier conversations, you said that love is situational. I think by that you meant that a loving action in one situation might not be a loving action in another, yet the action might be the same. I wonder how far you would go with situationism. Let me be more specific. You say that love-itself is always nonviolent, that love never harms the one-loved. Yet, if love is situational, on occasion might it be that love demands violence, if the situation requires it? [*pointing intently with his finger for emphasis on each of the last five words*]

Adam: [*smiling*] I detect you are trying to trip me up again! I would say that violence is never loving and that, as a principle, love would always seek a way other than physical force or emotional duress. Whenever violence is used, there is damage to the integrity of the one on whom violence is used. That one, too, is a loved one. Violence is the failure to love. That is why love's virtue of no-harm is complementary to love's virtue of goodness. No-harm helps to set the parameters of goodness. In practical terms, to develop the virtue of no-harm requires vigilance in finding ways of resolving conflicts that do not require violence.

Barry: So to develop the virtue of love you call no-harm would require some diligence in learning nonviolent conflict resolution.

Adam: Yes it would.

Barry: [*slightly frowning*] Which in itself is quite demanding.

Adam: [*grinning*] I didn't say love as a guide to morals would be easy! That brings me to love's next virtue, which is courage. I'll save that for later.

Scene 2

Some time later. Seating area outside squash court Number 1, the back wall of which is glass to allow observation of games. Their court was double-booked and Barry and Adam decide to use the time watching others play while they chat.

Barry: I'm sorry we missed our game today.

Adam: Me too. Still, I've a bit of a sore shoulder from the last game we played.

Barry: [*laughing*] When you crashed into the wall. You don't want to do that too often!

Adam: Probably best that I give it a rest today.

Barry: At least we can talk about your book. [*pausing*] It interests me that you include courage as one of love's virtues. Courage is quintessentially the virtue of the warrior. That would seem to be the antithesis of love. It has always interested me that when Aristotle lists his virtues he includes courage, but finds no place for love. His culture was patriarchal, masculinist, and imbued with martial virtue. Taking your very different approach to virtue, I'm surprised you give this concession.

Adam: I'm glad you have raised this. It has been a common misunderstanding of love that love is very weak, mostly soft, and can be applied by weak people. Actually, it is the reverse! To love requires enormous amounts of courage. It's the same with pacifism. People commonly make the mistake of thinking that pacifism is really passivism—the weak are passive, only the strong are active. In a similar way, it is a misunderstanding to think that love is passive and a soft option. To always make a choice for love requires as much courage as to make a choice for violence.[4]

Barry: Didn't Gandhi say something similar with regard to his use of nonviolence and the training of his satyagrahis.[5]

Adam: Yes, he required training in nonviolence as much as an army requires training in violence. Gandhi assumed that to become nonviolent meant to take the violence of the aggressor upon yourself. Love is willing to suffer violence, to absorb violence, and so, ultimately, to end violence. That requires great courage. [*pause*] But, courage is also required in other than life and death situations. To love also always runs the risk of rejection or

failure. To suffer rejection is a very powerful emotion. To fail is often an
unbearable prospect. And so, for some, it is better not to love than to run
the risk of rejection or failure and to suffer the consequences.

Barry: I can see that sometimes love requires courage. Yet, surely not all love
is courageous?

Adam: Another good observation! It brings me to something else I will point to
with regard to love's virtues: some of its virtues are more important
with different ways of loving.

Barry: You mean that not all of love's virtues apply equally to each of your
different ways of loving?

Adam: Take courage and affection, for example. You recall that I will argue
that affection is the homiest of the ways of loving. By and large, as
such, it does not require much courage to engage in.

Barry: [*smiling*] How much courage does it take to love your dog?

Adam: You might think not much at all. But, I do know some who, having
loved a dog, suffer terribly when the dog dies. They vow never to have
another animal companion. It is too painful when you lose them. So,
even affection for a companion non-human animal requires at least
some courage. At times, friendship, too, requires courage—perhaps to
defend a friend's honor or reputation—just as at times erosic love requires courage, when the lover is a mirror to the loved one to allow him
to see himself more clearly. Agapic love, in the face of great suffering
requires courage to be with the one who suffers, as well as in seeking to
alleviate her suffering. In fact, this virtue of courage is closely associated with love's virtue of fairness. As you correctly suggest, fairness
is how I will describe justice—after John Rawls.[6]

Barry: Justice is such a complex concept. I like that you have simplified it to
some extent as John Rawls did. Yet, in the popular mind, love and justice are often seen as opposites. If you do the loving action, you may
not be doing that which is most just. If you pursue justice, you may
have to abandon love. That "love is blind" is different from the way that
"justice is blind." The lover often refuses to see the faults and errors of
the loved one. Justice maintains a complete impartiality. These two
ideas seem to be at odds. I would be interested to see how you deal with
this popular conception.

Adam: I grant that in erosic love or friendship, fairness may not be a primary
virtue. Yet, I think you can see its requirement clearly with agapic love
and affection. Compassion and altruism are often sparked by a perceived
lack of justice. People suffer because life is too often unfair, unjust. To

seek justice is a compassionate response to injustice. So, rather than see justice as the opposite of love, or excluding love, I will make the argument that the virtue of justice as fairness is an essential virtue of love.

Barry: You mention fairness related to affection.

Adam: Yes, any mother knows that the affection she feels for her children requires the virtue of fairness. She needs to be fair to all her children.

Barry: That's often difficult! Parents do sometimes have more affection for one child than the others. Are you suggesting that affection needs the counter-balancing weight of fairness.

Adam: Yes.

Barry: Your next virtue?

Adam: Kindness with gentleness. Love of every sort is kind. Lovingkindness is a key component of morality.[7]

Barry: Kindness is one of those virtues that we know when we experience it or when we show it, yet I think difficult to put into words. I assume you are going to try?

Adam: I will do my best, though you are right in your observations. There are narrow ways to think about kindness and very broad ways. In the broadest terms, some writers think that kindness alone is a sufficient guide to morals.[8] These writers think of kindness as the same as love, particularly as agapic love or compassion. I think their argument is quite strong. Much that I will say in my book about love they say about kindness. However, I will use kindness in a narrower sense as one of the virtues of love.

Barry: And kindness on your narrow definition is . . .

Adam: My definition is that virtue of showing consideration, generosity and open-heartedness to others. Kindness is very soft, perhaps the most tender of love's virtues. Kindness as an action is love in motion toward the Other in tenderness to reduce the distance between lover and Other in a warm and mild way. If I can change my metaphor . . .

Barry: [*interrupting with a smile*] I hope you won't in your book. Didn't you learn in school not to mix your metaphors?

Adam: [*slightly raising eyebrows and sighing gently*] Kindness is soothing oil that reduces friction and makes relationships run smoothly. I do not know of anyone who is not warmed, and often surprised by kindness. To receive kindness makes you happy. Even thoughts of kind acts make you involuntarily smile. To act kindly has the same effect. Kindness is essential to well-being. The world would be better for more kindness.

Barry: [*smiling*] I can't disagree.

Adam: Kindness is linked clearly to gentleness.

Barry: Are they not the same?

Adam: I think kindness and gentleness are closely related but are not the same. Kindness will always be gentle, but whereas kindness is the action itself, gentleness is the manner in which all actions should be carried out. So, it is appropriate to say "kind and gentle." That is not a tautology. The difference would be this: a passer-by who sees a small child fall off her bike would act kindly if she picked up the bike and asked the child if she was hurt. The way in which she would help the child to her feet would be with gentleness.

Barry: I guess you could speak of a gentle breeze, but you would not speak of a kind breeze.

Adam: Yes, there is the difference. To develop a loving character would be to practice acts of kindness in a gentle manner. Love is always kind. Love is always gentle.

Barry: As I listen to your description of love's virtues, it reminds me of those virtues that were thought of as virtues of the home, or the feminine virtues, of the Victorian period. The Victorians saw a clear difference between the work of worldly affairs and that which happened in the home. The male of the family worked in the harsh world of commerce or industry where a different set of virtues were needed than in the soft world of the family. In industry kindness is not a virtue. In the competitive world of business, gentleness might well be a vice! I could hear a criticism of your list of virtues that they would simply not work in public life.

Adam: Piero Rerrucci calls this "the eternal feminine—love and tenderness and warmth."[9] I can understand your criticism. At first glance, it does seem that love and tenderness would be ill-equipped to deal with the harshness of the world of realpolitik. However, from my perspective, the fact that these virtues have been excluded from public life is part of the problem. We have often assumed that the necessities of the public world need a set of more robust, masculine virtues.

Barry: [*interrupting*] Not unlike Aristotle's list of public male virtues— basically warrior virtues.

Adam: Yes. Aristotle had no place for gentleness or kindness. I will suggest that as love guides morals, love's virtues exercised in public life would make all the difference in the world.

Barry: There are some foundational ideas lurking here about human nature and socialization. If human beings are naturally competitive and aggressive, then your softer virtues—if I may call them that—would likely not be helpful. Even if human beings are naturally kind, then society soon requires a different way to live in order to get by—survival of the fittest, perhaps—and the most fit are those who know how to fight.

Adam: It was the Hobbesian assumption that, naturally, human life is a war of all against all.[10] Civilization is the way to moderate the brutalities of nature. In different forms this idea has held sway right up to our own day. Civilization has often to be harsh to deal with the brutality of nature. Even Rousseau, who rejected this view of nature in favor of something more benevolent, assumed that civilization would teach us the harsher realities of life.

Barry: That supports my point. Most philosophers of the modern period seem to agree that given life as it is, love would not be adequate for the public sphere.

Adam: The criticism you suggest is much the same that has been leveled at the feminist ethics of care.

Barry: And care is your next virtue I presume. But, tell me, how do the feminists deal with the critique?

Adam: The feminist ethicists challenge traditional liberal ethics as too individualistic. Ethics is, they argue, about relationships, and fundamentally the relationship of care.[11] [*pausing*] I am very interested in the ethics of care and see its emphasis very close to love as a guide to morals. But, as with kindness, which can be seen as the primary category subsuming other ideas under a broad umbrella, in my book I will take a narrower view of care—care is one of the virtues of love. A lover is one who cares for the Other. To care is to provide what is necessary for the well-being of the Other.

Barry: Is the level of care to be exercised the same for all whom we love? I can see that you might argue that the lover is always gentle, always kind, but it seems to me that "to care for" has many possible levels.

Adam: That's a great observation. Do you remember in an earlier discussion I said that there are expanding circles of loving concern? It is appropriate to see care in those terms. The ethicists of care say that care is not universal.

Barry: In what sense?

Adam: In the sense that we couldn't possibly care for everyone alike. It is for that reason that the ethicists of care reject a universal love as a guide to morals. To love all universally, in the sense of caring for all alike, is impossible. I agree with that analysis. Care can only be exercised for those with who I am in a direct relationship. I can care for my child in a way that I cannot care for a child in India. We can care for folk in our neighborhood in a way we can't for folk in Switzerland.

Barry: For you, then, care as a virtue is more limited than a virtue that is universalized.

Adam: Yes. Nonetheless, to love is to care. It depends on what form love takes as to the level of care to be given. You care for a friend in a different way than you care for your spouse, in a different way than you care for your colleague.

Scene 3

The game they were watching ends, and the two philosophers make their way to the main exit. As they leave their breath is visible as they talk in the crisp winter air.

Barry: I am interested in hearing about other virtues of love you consider.

Adam: After care, I will consider faithfulness. Again, it is a virtue that is more suited to some ways of loving rather than others.

Barry: I can immediately see that. My guess is that you will talk about faithfulness mostly in the context of erosic love. There is a long tradition of lovers being faithful and relationships failing because of infidelity.

Adam: Faithfulness is also an appropriate virtue to friendship, though in a different way to erosic love. Erosic love is usually monogamous. We discussed that before. We tend to have one life partner at a time, but probably have several good friends simultaneously.

Barry: Tell me, why is faithfulness so important in a loving relationship?

Adam: In part, it is either explicit (in marriage vows, for instance) or implicit in monogamous relationships. I have posed the same question to my students on a number of occasions. Mostly, students take a dim view of cheating.

Barry: And cheating in this context means being unfaithful to a present girlfriend or boyfriend.

Adam: Even though there is much "hooking up" on a college campus—which I take to mean fairly casual sex without any commitment—when a relationship is formed, there is an implicit expectation of faithfulness.

Barry: But, that doesn't really answer the question why faithfulness is important. You are merely describing an expectation.

Adam: I agree in one sense. But, expectations in a social context need to be met, more or less, for social cohesion to exist. So to get by in our culture, there needs to be at least a rudimentary ability to be faithful. Yet, there is something more important. It is that love is often proved over a long time. For love to grow, deepen, and develop, love needs time. Over time love is tested, and in the testing the lover needs to grow the virtue of faithfulness.[12]

Barry: I assume in your book you will look at this in more detail? I'm thinking particularly about faithfulness is situations of abuse. You must have read cases where a woman is told to remain faithful to an abusive partner. Couldn't that be said to be a way of teaching the abused women faithfulness? And who'd want to endorse that!

Adam: Of course you are right. In cases of abuse, I don't think faithfulness is due to the abuser. I am just giving you the lay of the land. [*pausing*] Where trust is irretrievably broken, there is no requirement to be faithful. In fact, I link faithfulness to my next virtue, that of trust.

Barry: This is a big one. It is not always easy to trust another, especially when there has been a breach of trust.

Adam: That is why I link trust to faithfulness. They are like the flip side of a coin. If I demonstrate faithfulness to you as a friend, then you will more willing to trust me. By exercising faithfulness to you, I help you develop the virtue of trust. In being faithful, I show myself to be a trustworthy person.

Barry: In an erosic relationship, I can see the mutuality of trust and faithfulness taking place. As we are faithful to each other, we build trust.

Adam: Faithfulness and trust fulfill each other.

Barry: Will you say anything in your book about when faithfulness and trust are broken?

Adam: That subject needs a book of its own! But, I will suggest that, as with all aspects of the virtue of love, these two are developed gradually and slowly over time. Each day brings opportunities to be faithful. Each new situation is a challenge for trust to take place. If a partner is unfaithful, yet wants the relationship to continue, then trust will be rebuilt only slowly as the partners continue in faithfulness. Other virtues will need to be exercised.

Barry: Like gentleness and kindness.

Adam: And fairness and courage. This demonstrates how interconnected all the of love's virtues are. They together make up love as the supreme virtue. To comprehend love, we need to consider it in its many facets. Of course, a central virtue to prevent a relationship breakdown is forgiveness.

Barry: [*smiling*] You know I have a bit of an aversion to forgiveness.

Adam: [*looking puzzled*] How so?

Barry: Like many of my generation, I grew up in a religious context that overemphasized how bad we human beings are. We were made to feel terrible about ourselves.

Adam: [*laughing*] The "miserable worm" treatment!

Barry: You can laugh, but at the time, it was no laughing matter. God was said to rule the planet with a wrathful vengeance. Even your best was not good enough. In fact, your best was so tainted with sin it needed to be purified though suffering.

Adam: [*grimacing*] Ouch!

Barry: And that was the context in which forgiveness was spoken. When I discarded religion in my twenties, I wanted nothing more to do with that unhealthy emphasis on human badness and the need to be forgiven.

Adam: I see your point. The religious emphasis of forgiveness is that I, the sinner, need to be forgiven for my wrongs. It is about my escape from personal badness.

Barry: If that is what you mean, I want nothing to do with it!

Adam: Well, let me reassure you that that is far from what I will talk about in my book. I will look at it from the other side, so to speak—from the side of the one doing the forgiving. Forgiveness, as a virtue, is the lover letting go of the wrongs, real and perceived, of the loved one. It is about the process of bringing reconciliation when relationships go wrong. Forgiveness means that offense will not destroy a relationship.

Barry: Offense is a tricky idea! I have noticed that, on occasion, someone will take great offense where none was intended. And, on other occasions, someone will take no offense when the Other was being deeply offensive and intended to cause harm.

Adam: That is a good observation. Psychologically, forgiveness is about the one offended letting go of the offense and freeing onseself from bitterness and brooding. This is true when offense was intended and when no offense was intended. It is the one who perceives offense who suffers. Forgiveness allows that person to move on and exercise love again.

Barry: Are you saying that to love requires the virtue of forgiveness?

Adam: Yes. Without forgiveness, from the first time that offense arises, love will be unable to function.

Barry: Are you also saying that forgiveness is only about the one forgiving and is not about the one forgiven?

Adam: Not exactly. I am suggesting that forgiveness is psychologically beneficial to the one loving. However, when a genuine wrong has occurred— let's say I betray your trust by telling a third party something you have asked me to hold in confidence, which causes you harm—forgiveness makes room for reconciliation. Chances are, that I, too, will feel bad about the betrayal of trust. It will be hanging over me like a dark cloud and our relationship will be spoiled. By your exercising the virtue of forgiveness and communicating it to me, our friendship has space to grow again. It is a "win-win." We both benefit.

Barry: Something has always bothered me about the concept of forgiveness. It seems so unreasonable. If I have truly hurt someone, what right have I to expect forgiveness for my wrong? Surely, justice requires that, in some way, I live with the consequences of my action?

Adam: You are correct. In that sense, forgiveness is not reasonable. Forgiveness abandons the kind of justice that requires you to "get what you deserve." Forgiveness makes way for loving reconciliation. Forgiveness is merciful.

Barry: Carry on with your list of love's virtues.

Adam: If you recall, I am not suggesting that my list is exhaustive. By now you will also realize that all of love's virtues are interconnected and the lines between them are blurred. My next virtue is mindfulness. I would also consider this aspect to include awareness, or attentiveness. It would be a state of being present for the loved one, giving her your attention.[13]

Barry: I see. The opposite would be to listen to someone without really hearing them. I suppose, that is what being absent-minded is.

Adam: Yes, it is quite a skill to exist in the present moment without either being locked into the past or the future. In a relationship, if I am focused on what happened between us in the past, it will disable good communication in the present. If my mind is running away into what might happen next, then I am not truly present in the relationship. Of love's many aspects, mindfulness requires daily attention, and moment-by-moment focus in any interaction.

Barry: This section of your book—love's practice—must, I assume, be practical. Will you give your readers any help on how to develop mindfulness?

Adam: There are some very helpful skills developed mostly in Eastern philosophy related to meditation and mindfulness, and much has been written about it in recent years. I will give a broad overview and suggest a number of useful resources for readers to help them develop the virtue.[14]

Barry: You mean something like sitting or walking meditation practices from the Zen tradition?

Adam: Yes. Simple breathing meditation where the practitioner learns to focus only on the breath is wonderful mindfulness training. This leads me to my next virtue, that of thankfulness, though that one word hardly covers all I mean. It is that virtue of celebratory joy in the goodness of life itself. Love is the great celebration of life. Being thankful for whom we are and all that we have also frees us to love the Other. Thankfulness is a very happy virtue. Thankfulness is also linked to non-possessiveness.

Barry: I can see that grasping and controlling are love's enemies. The lover so wants to possess the Other that he smothers the Other and loses him.

Adam: How true! I have seen it in parent-child relationships, in erosic love, and in friendships. To grip too tightly spoils love. Yet, it is such a temptation. When love is intense, the lover wants more than ever to be with the Other. The thought that the Other may have a life outside of that intense relationship can be too much to bear. Jealousies arise and cause the lover to hold even tighter. The Other rebels against the pressure and things go from bad to worse.

Barry: If I recall correctly from our previous conversations, you would see this as a corruption of love.

Adam: Yes. Jealousy and control are not part of love-itself, but are accretions of attitudes and feelings other than love. It is why lovers need to practice letting go. Lovers need to give the Other space to grow and be themselves. Lovers need, at times, to realize that the love relationship is changing and that the Other needs to find different relationships. Friendships are of this kind as well as erosic relationships.

Barry: I would say this is the case supremely for parents as their children mature. It is the parent's failure to let go of the late-teenager that is a cause of so much friction. But, how hard it is to do!

Adam: That is why all virtues require small steps. In letting-go of our children by increasing their freedom—at first in small things and then in larger—the parent gradually gets used to letting go.

Barry: This is one of the great insights of Buddhist philosophy. I assume you will mention this in your book.

Adam: Of course! In Buddhism's Four Noble Truths, it is attachment that is the cause of suffering. Much Buddhist practice is learning the way of non-attachment and letting-go.[15]

Barry: By my count, you must be at the end of your list of love's virtues.

Adam: My final virtue is moderation.

Barry: Good! I have been waiting to see what you will say about this. It seems to me that moderation is not what is found in most ways of loving. Erosic love, for example, is far from moderate. Compassion, too, is often intense, immoderate. How can you be moderate when you see a starving child?

Adam: But, that is the point exactly! Love can be so intense that love needs the virtue of moderation to prevent its excesses. I'm sure you have heard of compassion burnout. A sensitive person can feel such strong feelings of compassion that the emotion threatens to overwhelm. I once knew a student who became so sensitized to the sufferings of non-human animals that the thought of their suffering incapacitated him. The student couldn't think about anything else. He stopped eating.

Barry: Not just meat you mean?

Adam: He stopped eating everything. Fortunately, with some good philosophical reflection, the student was able to find balance again. He still felt deeply for the plight of abused animals, but was able to channel his compassion in helpful ways. He learned the virtue of moderation. This is true for all the ways of loving.

Barry: Even erosic love?

Adam: [*grinning*] Perhaps, especially erosic love! Of course, during the first flush of romance, nothing would bring a temperate view. That intense stage of the relationship lasts for a short time anyway. Lovers need to develop the virtue of moderation for their love to last and deepen.

Barry: So that's it then! It's quite a comprehensive list of virtues related to love. And that will also be the end of your book.

Adam: I will take my readers on a journey considering the ways we love, the problems with the ways we love, the contemplation of love-itself, how love is a useful guide to morals, and how through daily habit we can build the virtues of love leading to more loving lives.

Barry: [*blowing warm air on his fingers*] I'm freezing. Can we go inside?

Scene 4

At the end of the same day. Barry and the Dean are standing chatting outside the Dean's suite of offices. Adam is walking by and Barry calls him over.

Barry: Adam, I was just talking to the Dean about your new book.

The Dean: I hear that it's near completion Adam. Barry was explaining your ideas, but I'd rather hear them from you. [*looking at her watch, slightly flustered*] I don't have very long, but give me a quick summary. Another book on ethics—I presume money and sex? [*playfully raising her eyebrow*]

Adam: [*nervously laughing*] Money, sex, and everything else! Ethics is about the way we live, and asks the question, "What is a good life?" I give one particular answer, suggesting that we should live a loving life. Love is a guide to morals.

The Dean: How would romance guide our morals?

Adam: [*frowning slightly*] Love is more than romance. I argue that love in all its complexity—erosic love, friendship, affection, and agapic love—is the great good of human life. Even though, at times, our love is disappointed, or incomplete, or less than we would want it to be, still we long for a loving life. It matches our embodiment. Like all mammals, we are social animals, and our highest relationships are loving ones. The loves we experience lead us to the contemplation of love-itself: the fullness and perfection of love.

The Dean: [*a little doubtfully*] But is it practical?

Adam: Very much so! As our experience of love leads us to the contemplation of love-itself, so contemplation of love-itself leads us to the habits and virtues of a more loving life.

The Dean: Very good! [*looking at her watch again, and beginning to walk away*] Well I must fly. [*looking over her shoulder*] So, the punch line is what?

Adam: A loving life is a good life. [*pausing momentarily*] The world would be better for more loving lives.

Act VII

EPILOGUE

Three months after their last conversation, Barry and Adam have just played the final point in a grueling six-match squash marathon. It is several minutes before either can speak. When they do, their words are in short bursts as they gasp for breath.

Barry: I've been meaning to ask about your book. Where are you up to?

Adam: All done and dusted! I sent the final manuscript to the publishers yesterday. I called it *Love as a Guide to Morals*.

Barry: That's great news! Which publishers?

Adam: Rodopi's, Value Inquiry Book Series went for it to be placed in its special series, Ethical Theory and Practice, after some careful negotiation [*picking up the little black ball from the far corner of the court*]. I did make a few changes since we last talked about it. I decided to write in dialogue format.

Barry: In the steps of Plato! You're continuing the great tradition, then.

Adam: That was part of it. But, as we had our long chats on the squash court, it seemed natural to write a conversation between two fictional philosophers as they discuss a book one of them is about to write.

Barry: Nice twist!

Adam: Of course, it's not quite our dialogue, and I changed our names.

Barry: [*playfully laughing*] To protect the innocent, I presume? So, what names did you give these fictional philosophers?

Adam: Something nondescript. Larry and Andy.

Barry: [*shrugging*] Fancy a beer? I'm ready for one.

Adam: [*opening the door to leave the squash court*] Lead on MacDuff!

Barry: [*scratching his beard*] You mean surely, "Lay on McDuff"? The phrase you used is misquoted from Shakespeare. In the Scottish Play, Act 5, Scene 8, Macbeth says to McDuff . . .

Adam: [*interrupting with exasperation*] Whatever!

THE END

.

ENDNOTES

Preface

1. Iris Murdoch, *Metaphysics as a Guide to Morals* (New York: Allen Lane, Penguin, 1993).

Act I: Love and Morality

1. Good introductory texts for metaphysics (ontology, the question of being) and episte-mology (the question of knowledge) include Duncan Pritchard, *What Is the Thing Called Knowledge?* (New York: Routledge, 2006) and Brian Garrett, *What Is This Thing Called Metaphysics?* (New York: Routledge, 2006).
2. A good introduction to aesthetics is George Dickie's *Introduction to Aesthetics: An Analytical Approach* (Oxford: Oxford University Press, 1997).
3. This refers to ethics, which will be the subject of the conversations that follow. There has been some debate as to whether ethics and morality are the same thing. Mo-rality is sometimes seen in a narrowly defined way as actions of rightness or wrongness and ethics in a broader, more theoretical sense, as the sum total of the way one lives. However, in this book, I am assuming that morality, moral philos-ophy, and ethics all refer to the same branch of philosophical inquiry, and the book is an attempt to answer the basic, yet most important question, "How should we live?"
4. In Greek mythology, the wandering Odysseus has to pass between two cliffs that har-bor two monsters, Scylla and Charybdis. Charybdis was daughter of Mother Earth and Poseidon and had been hurled by Zeus into the sea. Three times daily she now sucked down huge amounts of water and spat it out again. Scylla was the daughter of Hecate Crataeis and has been changed into a dog-like monster with six heads and twelve feet. She would attack and swallow sailors whole! See Ro-bert Graves, *The Greek Myths* (London: Folio Society, 1996), pp. 646–666.
5. For an introduction to how to make an argument, see Richard Paul and Linda Elder, *The Thinkers Guide to Fallacies* (Dillon Beach, Calif.: Foundation for Critical Thinking, 2004); and *The Miniature Guide to Understanding the Foundations of Ethical Reasoning* (Dillon Beach, Calif.: Foundation for Critical Thinking, 2005).
6. René Descartes, "Meditation Two" in *Meditations on First Philosophy* (Indianapolis, Ind.: Bobbs-Merrill, 1960/1641). Descartes held that if we doubt everything that can be doubted, we are left with knowledge. The one thing I cannot doubt is that I am thinking about the possibility of doubt. My thinking/doubting is the knowledge that I, therefore, exist. To doubt all that can be doubted became a foundational principle in modern epistemology.
7. Lydia B. Amir has an interesting comment in this regard: "In the latter decades of the twentieth century, the pendulum appears to have swung back to a richer and more ambitious conception of philosophical ethics: in the words of a recent commenta-tor, philosophy began to be 'freed from an overly restrictive conception of the task' and to refocus their attention on the fundamental questions about how to live that have always given the subject its significant appeal" "Morality, Psychology, Philosophy," *Philosophical Practice*, 1:1 (2005), p. 53.

8. Plato, *The Republic*, trans. Desmond Lee (London: Penguin, 1987); Augustine, *City of God*, trans. Henry Bettensen (London: Penguin, 2003); and Karl Marx and Friedrich Engels, *The Communist Manifesto*, trans. Samuel Moore (London: Penguin, 1967).

9. I agree with James Griffin when he says, "much of our moral vocabulary in English has a certain—to my mind wrongheaded—model of moral relations built into it etymologically: the terms 'ought,' 'should,' 'duty,' 'obligation,' 'retribution,' 'merit,' 'rights,' contract,' all come originally from commerce or commercially oriented law, and have to do with owing, paying, binding, and so on," *Value Judgment: Improving Our Ethical Beliefs* (Oxford: Clarendon Press, 1996), p. 4.

10. Gandhi and King often use "love," "nonviolence," and "*ahimsa*" interchangeably. Good writings by Gandhi and King are: Gandhi, *The Essential Gandhi, an Anthology* , ed. Louis Fischer (New York: Random House, 2002); *Gandhi's Experiments with Truth: Essential Writings by and about Mahatma Gandhi*, ed. Richard L. Johnson (Lanham, Md.: Lexington Books, 2006); and *Non-Violent Resistance (Satyagraha)* (Mineola, N.Y.: Dover, 2001); and Martin Luther King Jr., *A Testament of Hope: The Essential Writings of Martin Luther King Jr.*, ed. James Melvin (San Francisco, Calif.: Harper & Row, 1986).

11. Iris Murdoch, *The Sovereignty of Good* (New York: Routledge, 1970), p. 45.

12. Irving Singer, *The Nature of Love 1: Plato to Luther* (Cambridge, Mass.: The MIT Press, 2009); *The Nature of Love 2: Courtly and Romantic* (Cambridge, Mass.: The MIT Press, 2009); *The Nature of Love 3: The Modern World* (Cambridge, Mass.: The MIT Press, 2009). See also Plato, *Philosophy of Love: A Partial Summing-Up* (Cambridge, Mass.: The MIT Press, 2009) and *The Pursuit of Love* (Baltimore, Md.: Johns Hopkins University Press, 1994).

13. Alan Soble, *Eros, Agape, and Philia: Readings in the Philosophy of Love* (New York: Paragon House Publishers, 1989); *The Structure of Love* (New Haven, London: Yale University Press, 1990); and *The Philosophy of Sex and Love*, 2nd edition, ed. John K. Roth and Frederick Sontag (St. Paul, Minn.: Paragon House, 2008).

14. See for example, Thomas Lewis, Fari Amini, and Richard Lannon, *A General Theory of Love* (New York: Vintage Books, 2000); Erich Fromm, *The Art of Loving* (New York: Harper Perennials, 1956).

15. Among a few notable exceptions on love and morality are Pitirim A.Sorokin, *The Ways and Power of Love: Types, Factors, and Techniques of Moral Transformation* (Radnor, Penn.: Templeton Foundation Press, 1982); and Stephen G. Post, *Unlimited Love: Altruism, Compassion and Service* (Philadelphia, Penn.: Templeton Foundation Press, 2003).

16. On how we are shaped by culture and history, see Hans Georg Gadamer, *Truth and Method* (London: Sheed & Ward, 1975); Gadamer with David E. Linge, *Philosophical Hermeneutics* (Berkeley: University of California Press,1976). On the way communities shape the kind of people we are and the kinds of values we hold, see Daniel Bell, *Communitarianism and Its Critics* (Oxford: Clarendon Press, 1993). Alasdair MacIntyre's philosophical project can be viewed as the acknowledgement that moral concepts are not disembodied ideas, but "embodied in and are partially constitutive of forms of social life." See his *A Short History of Ethics: A History of Moral Philosophy from the Homeric Age to the Twentieth Century* (London: Routledge, 1967), p.1. In other words, morality is rooted in tradition. "Truths" are always embodied and need to be understood from within the tradition that gives birth to them. MacIntyre works out his theory in his great

trilogy juxtaposing the Aristotelian tradition (largely as interpreted by Thomas Aquinas) with the universalist claims of Enlightenment rationality. See *After Virtue: A Study in Moral Theory* (London: Gerald Duckworth, 1985); *Whose Justice? Which Rationality?* (London: Duckworth, 1988); and *Three Rival Versions of Moral Inquiry* (London: Duckworth, 1990).

17. See Griffin, *Value Judgment*, pp. 8–12.

18. Pamela Sue Anderson makes such an observation in formulating a feminist philosophy of religion in *A Feminist Philosophy of Religion: The Rationality and Myths of Religious Belief* (Oxford and Malden: Blackwell, 1998).

19. Prima facie moral axioms are basic ethical beliefs that are not reached through argument. For some philosophers, such as Thomas Reid in the eighteenth century and George Edward Moore in the early twentieth, basic moral beliefs are self-evident. See Sabine Roeser, *Moral Emotions and Intuitions* (New York: Palgrave Macmillan, 2011), pp. 12. David Ross listed seven basic ethical beliefs he called "prima facie duties": fidelity, reparation, justice, beneficence, gratitude, self-improvement, and nonmaleficence. See *The Right and the Good* (Oxford: Oxford University Press, 2002), pp. 20–21.

20. "The heart has its reasons about which reason knows nothing." Blaise Pascal, *Pensées*, ed. and trans., Roger Ariew (Indianapolis: Hackett, 2005), p. 216.

21. See John Macmurray, *Reason and Emotion*, 2nd ed. (Amherst, N.Y.: Humanity Books, 1992); and Robert Solomon, *The Passions: Emotions and the Meaning of Life* (Indianapolis, Ind.: Hackett, 1993) and *Not Passions Slave: Emotions and Choice* (Oxford: Oxford University Press, 2003); and Martha C. Nussbaum, *Upheavals of Thought: The Intelligence of Emotions* (New York: Cambridge University Press, 2001).

22. For two good introductions to the validity and truth value of moral statements see Mary Midgley, *Can't We Make Moral Judgments?* (New York: St. Martin's Press, 1993); and Simon Blackburn, *Being Good: A Short Introduction to Ethics* (Oxford: Oxford University Press, 2001).

23. David Hume deals with sympathy in the second part of *A Treatise of Human Nature* (London: Penguin, 1969) and in *An Enquiry Concerning the Principles of Morals* (Indianapolis: Hackett, 1983).

24. See Adam Smith, *The Theory of Moral Sentiments* (Mineola, N.Y.: Dover Publications). Smith begins his treatise: "How selfish soever man may be supposed, there are evidently some principles in his nature, which interest him in the fortune of others, and render their happiness necessary to him, though he derives nothing from it, except the pleasure of seeing it. Of this kind is pity or compassion, the emotion which we feel for the misery of others, when we either see it, or are made to conceive it in a very lively manner. . . . The greatest ruffian, the most hardened violator of the laws of society, is not altogether without it" p. 3.

25. On the free will-determinism debate see Thomas Pink, *Free Will: A Very Short Introduction* (Oxford: Oxford University Press, 2004).

26. See, for example, James Rachels and Stuart Rachels, *The Elements of Moral Philosophy*, sixth edition (New York: McGraw Hill, 2010); Simon Blackburn, *Ethics: A Very Short Introduction* (Oxford: Oxford University Press, 2001); Robert C. Solomon, *On Ethics and Living Well* (Belmont: Wadsworth/Thomson, 2006).

27. For an introduction and Kant's major ethical writings see, *Ethical Philosophy*, trans. James W. Ellington (Indianapolis: Hackett, 1983); Roger Scruton, *Kant: A Very*

Short Introduction (Oxford: Oxford University Press, 2001); and Onora O'Neil, "Kantian Ethics," in Peter Singer, *A Companion to Ethics* (Cambridge: Blackwell, 1991).

28. Fletcher says, love is "goodwill at work in partnership with reason," and "pinned down to its precise meaning, Christian love is benevolence, literally, Goodwill." *Situation Ethics: The New Morality* (Philadelphia, Penn.: Westminster Press, 1966), pp. 69 and 105, respectively.

29. Ibid., pp. 167–168.

30. Søren Kierkegaard discusses the commandment to love; he contrasts spontaneous love with a duty to love. The duty to love is not dependent on the Other (who may be unlovely), whereas spontaneous love is dependent on continued appreciation of the good in the Other. When the good fades, then so does love. Love as a duty is, therefore, the most free kind of love, according to Kierkegaard. Kant also speaks about the command to love. He makes a distinction between rational and pathological love. It is the former that is moral love. See *Works of Love: Kierkegaards's Writing*, trans. Howard V. Hong and Edna H. Hong (Princeton, N.J.:Princeton University Press, 1962), pp. 29–43.

Act II
Love's Complexity

1. On ideas that are conceptually inaccessible, see G. E. Moore, *Principia Ethica* (Amherst: Prometheus Books, 1988); and Rudolf Otto, *The Idea of the Holy: An Inquiry into the Non-Rational Factor in the Idea of the Divine and Its Relation to the Rational*, trans. John W. Harvey (London: Oxford University Press, 1950). Love is very like Moore's conception of goodness. For Moore, goodness is not an amalgam derived from other ideas. Goodness is rather like the concept of "yellow." Yellow is understood by primitive pointing to: "The color of that is yellow." So we learn the color. Goodness and love are like that: it is impossible to say exactly what they are, but we learn goodness by having goodness pointed out to us: Goodness is that feeling; goodness is that activity. And so, that which you feel is love; that which you see the friend doing for the other friend is love. When Otto speaks of the holy, he says that, "it remains inexpressible . . . in the sense that it completely eludes apprehension in terms of concepts" (p. 5). Yet, we know the holy when we come across it. Love is like that.

2. Søren Kierkegaard said about love, "Something that is in its total richness is essentially inexhaustible is also in its smallest work essentially indescribable just because essentially it is totally present everywhere and essentially cannot be described." *Works of Love*, p. 3. Nonetheless, he went on to write almost 600 pages on love!

3. On Augustine, see Hannah Arendt, Joanna Vecchiarelli Scott, and Judith Chelius Stark, *Love and Saint Augustine* (Chicago, Ill.: The University of Chicago Press, 1996). Arendt quotes Augustine's *Eighty-three Different Questions*: "To love is indeed nothing else that to crave something for its own sake" and love is "A kind of motion, and all motion is toward something," p. 9.

4. Hannah Arendt comments, "since [a human being is] not self-sufficient and therefore always desires something outside himself, the question of who he is can only be resolved by the object of his desire and not, as the Stoics thought, by the suppression

of the impulse of desire itself: 'Such is each as is his love.' Strictly speaking, he who does not love and desire at all is a nobody." *Love and Saint Augustine*, p. 18.

5. M. Scott Peck has a similar understanding of love as motion toward. He terms it "extension of ourselves." He says, "when we extend ourselves, when we take an extra step or walk an extra mile, we do so in opposition to the inertia of laziness or the resistance of fear. Extension of ourselves or moving out against the inertia of laziness we call work. Moving out in the face of fear we call courage. Love then, is a form of work or a form of courage." *The Road Less Traveled: A New Way of Love, Traditional Values and Spiritual Growth* (New York: Touchstone, 1978), p. 120. See also, Nel Noddings, *A Feminine Approach to Ethics & Moral Education* (Berkeley: University of California Press, 2003). Noddings has a similar understanding of care. She says, "as I think about how I feel when I care, about what my frame of mind is, I see that my caring is always characterized by a move from the self" (ibid., p. 16).

6. See Hannah Arendt, *The Life of the Mind* (Orlando, Fla.: Harcourt, 1978), pp. 136 .

7. Attempts to define love by philosophers have been many and varied. In part, the variety exists because different philosophers have different ways of loving in mind. Yet, this accounts for the variation only in part, for even when the same way of loving is considered, understandings vary greatly. I include here a few attempts that require careful thought and attention. Harry Frankfurt says, "love is often understood as being, most basically, a response to the perceived worth of the beloved" in *The Reasons of Love* (Princeton, N.J.: Princeton University Press, 2004), p. 38. However, he suggests that we do not love because we perceive a value in the Other, but that because we love we place value in the Other. He suggest, "love is, most centrally a disinterested concern for the existence of what is loved, and for what is good for it" (ibid., p. 42). Robert Solomon goes back to a view expressed by Aristophanes in Plato's *Symposium*. Love is a shared self-identity and life is the process of finding "one's other half." Solomon says, "love is fundamentally the experience of redefining one's self in terms of the other." *About Love: Reinventing Romance for Our Times* (Indianapolis, Ind.: Hackett, 1994), pp. 24–25. His book is an analysis of how the process takes place. Mary Evans refuses to give a definition of love and looks instead at the ways love has been socially constructed as Western culture has changed. She says, "one of the many 'love troubles' of the West has always been that we have never been . . . entirely sure what we mean by love." *Love: An Unromantic Discussion* (Malden, Mass.: Blackwell, 2003), p. 26. Alan Soble, in *Eros, Agape, and Philia*, gives two definitions: "We define 'eros-style' love this way: x loves y because y has attractive or valuable qualities. In 'agape-style' love, then, x loves y independently of y's merit, and any merit of y's that plays a role in x's love is value that x attributes to or creates in y as a result of x's love," p. xxiv. Robert Wagoner suggests that "love" has many meanings. He identifies six different kinds of love in *The Meanings of Love: An Introduction to Philosophy of Love* (Westport: Praeger, 1997). Vladimir Sergeyevich Solovyov says simply, "the root meaning of love . . . consists in the acknowledgement of absolute significance for another being," in *The Meaning of Love*, trans. Thomas R. Beyer (West Stockbridge, Mass.: Lindisfarne Press, 1985), p. 87.

8. I borrow "un-selfing" from Iris Murdoch. See Floora Ruokonen, "Good, Self, and Un-selfing—Reflections on Iris Murdoch's Moral Philosophy," *Austrian Ludwig Wittgenstein Society* (2002), pp. 211–213.

9. For Freud, love of the Other is a form of mental well-being. According to Robert C. Solomon and Kathleen M. Higgins, "Freud argues that Romantic love is an outgrowth of our primary state of narcissism. Mental health requires the individual to move beyond narcissism and direct libido toward some external object. Thus love has a functional role in the mechanism of mental hygiene," in *The Philosophy of (Erotic) Love* (Lawrence: University Press of Kansas, 1991), p. 154. For a good critique of Freud on love see Pat Duffy Hutcheon, "Through a Glass Darkly: Freud's Concept of Love," in David Goicoechea, ed., *The Nature and Pursuit of Love: The Philosophy of Irving Singer* (Amherst, N.Y.: Prometheus Books, 1995), pp.183–195.

10. In Soble, *Eros, Agape, and Philia*, p. 86.

11. Nygren says, "there seems in fact to be no possibility of discovering any idea common to them both [agape and eros] which might serve as a starting-point for the comparison; for at every point the opposition between them makes itself felt" (ibid. p 93). For a more recent treatment that distinguishes agapic love from other kinds of love in such a way that only agapic love is "true" love, see Eric Silverman, *The Prudence of Love: How Possessing the Virtue of Love Benefits the Lover* (Lanham, Md.: Lexington Books, 2010). Silverman's account is a Neo-Thomistic version of love that sets the bar for true love very high. See my review and critique of his book: "Review of Eric Silverman, *The Prudence of Love: How Possessing the Virtue of Love Benefits the Lover*," *Teaching Philosophy* (March 2012).

12. See chart explaining the differences between eros and agape according to Nygren in Soble *Eros, Agape, and Philia*, p. 94.

13. Harry Frankfurt says, "it is widely presumed that for a person to love himself is so natural as to be more or less unavailable; but it is also widely presumed that this is not a good thing. . . . In their view, it is largely self-love that makes it impossible for us to devote ourselves sufficiently and in a suitable way—that is selflessly—to other things that we love or that it would be good for us to love. . . . The allegation that we are too deeply immersed in self-love is frequently offered, indeed, as identifying an almost insurmountable obstacle to our loving as we should," in *The Reasons of Love*, p. 71. Frankfurt sees self-love as "the purest of all modes of love" (ibid., p. 80). He suggests this because self-love meets the criteria he has developed for love: (1) being disinterested, (2) ineluctably personal,(3) identification with the beloved, and (4) the will is constrained.

14. See Appendix II, " Of Self Love" in *An Enquiry Concerning the Principles of Morals* (1751), in *David Hume: Moral Philosophy*, ed. Sayre-McCord, Geoffrey (Indianapolis, Ind.: Hackett, 2006): "The most obvious objection to the selfish hypothesis is, that, as it is contrary to common feeling and our most unprejudiced notions, there is required the highest stretch of philosophy to establish so extraordinary a paradox" (ibid., pp. 276–277).

15. The myth of Narcissus is delightfully told by Robert Graves in *The Greek Myths* I, pp. 267–269.

16. Perhaps, Ayn Rand (1905–1982), in her philosophy of objectivism, comes closest to a purely selfish moral philosophy. She argued that the moral life was in the pursuit of pure self-interest. Her philosophy is worked out chiefly in two novels: *The

Fountainhead (London: Harper Collins, 1994) and *Atlas Shrugged* (London: Penguin, 2007).

17. Though self-love is now a common idea in psychology, it was popularized by Peck in *The Road Less Traveled* and Leo Buscaglia in *Love* (New York: Ballentine Books, 1982). Their books arrived on the scene at roughly the same time and both were widely acclaimed. Peck defined love as "the will to extend one's self for the purpose of nurturing one's own or another spiritual growth" (p. 81). He said further, "this unitary definition of love includes self-love with love for the other. Since I am human and you are human, to love human beings means to love myself as well as you. . . . Indeed, as has been pointed out, we are incapable of loving another unless we love ourselves, just as we are incapable of teaching our children self-discipline unless we ourselves are self-disciplined" (pp. 82–82). For a critique of Peck and Buscaglia on self-love see Soble, *Eros, Agape, and Philia*, pp. xiii–xvii.

18. See Robert N. Bellah, *Habits of the Heart: Individualism and Commitment in American Life* (Early: University of California Press, 1985).

19. See Violet Staub De Laszlo, *The Basic Writings of C. G. Jung* (New York: The Modern Library, 1993). In *On the Nature of the Psyche* (New York: Modern Library: Random House, 1959), Jung says, "in this way the will [egocentric will/ego] as disposable energy, gradually subordinates itself to the stronger factor, namely to the new totality figure I call the self" (p. 120) and "the self comprises infinitely more than the ego . . ." (p. 122).

20. R. D. Laing, *The Divided Self* (London: Penguin, 1960). However, Laing deals specifically with the schizoid condition and his observations about when considering the "normal" self, where the "undivided self" is the healthy self-perception.

21. "For we know that the law is spiritual; but I am of the flesh, sold into slavery under sin. I do not understand my own actions. For I do not do what I want, but I do the very thing I hate. Now if I do what I do not want, I agree that the law is good. But in fact it is no longer I that do it, but sin that dwells within me. For I know that nothing good dwells within me, that is, in my flesh. I can will what is right, but I cannot do it. For I do not do the good I want, but the evil I do not want is what I do. Now if I do what I do not want, it is no longer I that do it, but sin that dwells within me" (Romans 7, NRSV). See Carl Rogers' breakthrough paper on the perception of self: "Some Observations on the Organization of Personality," *American Psychologist*, 2(1947), pp. 358–368; http://psychclassics.yorku.ca/Rogers/personality.htm (accessed 08 February 2012). Rogers argues that behavior is a function of self-perception rather than a function or organic or cultural factors. He analyses the kind of maladjusted self-perception that the ancient theologian describes.

22. See Martin Buber, *I and Thou*, trans. Walter Kaufman (New York: Touchtone, 1970). Buber is helpful is pointing out two ways human beings engage with the world: "I-You" relationships and "I-It" relationships. Loving relationships are always I-You relationships. If there is no "You" then it surely calls into question whether there is a love relationship.

23. Kierkegaard, *Works of Love*.

24. "Man is a political animal," Aristotle, *Politics*, 1278^{b}15.

25. Kant refers to masturbation in "Concerning Wanton Self-Abuse," in Part II of *The Metaphysics of Morals* (424). He sees it an "unnatural use and so misuse" and compares it to suicide. See *Ethical Philosophy: The Complete Texts of Grounding for the Metaphysics of Morals and Metaphysical Principles of Virtue (Part II of*

the Metaphysics of Morals) [1785, 1797], trans. James W. Ellington (Indianapolis: Hackett, 1983), p. 85.

26. I find only one passage in the Bible that seems to relate to (male) masturbation. Genesis 36:6–9 refers to the sin of Onan, who, by Jewish cultural tradition, was required to have children by his dead brother's wife. Instead, he "spilled his seed on the ground." There is no reference to female masturbation.

27. Aldous Huxley, *The Perennial Philosophy* (New York: Harper Perennial, 2009). Huxley took his title from Leibnitz, who coined the phrase *philosophia perennis*. Huxley gathered pertinent passages from the world's great religions and mysticisms to demonstrate their congruity, and included a running commentary about his findings. In a section on charity, he draws from the Christian mystical tradition, Judaism, Islam, and Eastern philosophies (pp. 80–96).

28. On act- and rule utilitarianism see Rachels and Rachels, *The Elements of Moral Philosophy*, pp. 118–119, and 122.

29. See Joseph F. Fletcher, *Situation Ethics*, p. 27. "It is possible to derive principles from whatever is the one universal norm . . . but not laws or rules. We cannot milk universals from a universal." The heart of Fletcher's thesis is this: "Christian situation ethics has only one norm or principle or law (call it what you will) that is binding and unexceptionable, always good and right regardless of the circumstances. That is 'love'—the agape of the summary commandments to love God and the neighbor. Everything else without exception, all laws and rules and principles and ideals and norms, are only contingent, only valid if they happen to serve love in any situation," p. 30. I differ from Fletcher, in that Fletcher can imagine the use of atomic weapons as loving, but I cannot. In the end, Fletcher betrays his own thesis in being merely a utilitarian.

30. The quote is: "the task of philosophy is to show what is nearest, what is deeply and obviously true but usually invisible" in *Metaphysics as a Guide to Morals*, p. 90.

Act III
Love's Appearance: Eros

1. Some argue that much philosophy is so saturated in masculinist, racist, classist terms that it is beyond redemption. The task is to start anew. This contrast can be seen in the different ways Pamela Sue Anderson and Grace Jantzen approach the philosophy of religion. Both are feminists committed to a critique of patriarchy, yet they produce different feminist philosophies of religion. Anderson takes the view that the old can be salvaged while introducing new conceptions. Jantzen argues that the project must be rebuilt without recourse to former categories of thinking. See Grace M. Jantzen, *Becoming Divine: Towards a Feminist Philosophy of Religion* (Bloomington and Indianapolis: Indiana University Press, 1999); and Pamela Sue Anderson, *A Feminist Philosophy of Religion* (Oxford: Blackwell, 1998).

2. "[The] threefold structure of untutored human-nature-as-it-happens-to-be, human-nature-as-it-could-be-if-it-realized-its-telos and the precepts of rational ethics as the means for the transition from one to the other remains central . . ." MacIntyre, *After Virtue*, p. 53.

3. "Every art and every investigation, and similarly every action and pursuit, is considered to aim at some good. Hence the good has been rightly defined as 'that at which all things aim'" Aristotle, *Nichomachean Ethics*, 1094a1). "[What] do we take to be

the end of political science—what is the highest of all practical goods? . . . [T]here is pretty general agreement. 'It is happiness' say both ordinary and cultured people; and they identify happiness with living well or doing well" (ibid, 1095a 18).

4. See Jean-Paul Sartre, *Being and Nothingness: An Essay in Phenomenological Ontology*, trans. Hazel Barnes (New York: Citadel Press, 2001), p. 55–78. See also Noddings' discussion of the use of the instrument in *Caring: A Feminine Approach to Ethics & Moral Education* (Berkeley: University of California Press, 2003), p. 4.

5. Max Weber, *The Sociology of Religion* (Boston: Beacon Press, 1993).

6. Immanuel Kant, *Critique of Pure Reason*, trans. J. M. D. Meiklejohn (Amherst, N.Y.: Prometheus Books, 1990), Bxxvi–xxvii.

7. Kant, *Critique of Practical Reason*, trans. Meiklejohn (Amherst, N.Y.: Prometheus, 1990).

8. Nel Noddings makes a similar claim for the human experience of caring. At the very least, the fact that each person is now alive means that they experienced at least rudimentary care as an infant. See *Caring*, p. 49.

9. Diagnostic criteria for 313.89 Reactive Attachment Disorder of Infancy or Early Childhood: "A. Markedly disturbed and developmentally inappropriate social relatedness in most contexts, beginning before age five years, as evidenced by either (1) persistent failure to initiate or respond in a developmentally appropriate fashion to most social interactions, as manifest by excessively inhibited, hyper vigilant, or highly ambivalent and contradictory responses (e.g., the child may respond to caregivers with a mixture of approach, avoidance, and resistance to comforting, or may exhibit frozen watchfulness); or (2) diffuse attachments as manifest by indiscriminate sociability with marked inability to exhibit appropriate selective attachments (e.g., excessive familiarity with relative strangers or lack of selectivity in choice of attachment figures)." American Psychiatric Association, *Diagnostic and Statistical Manual of Mental Disorders*, 4th ed. (Washington, D. C., 1994).

10. A. H. Maslow, "A Theory of Human Motivation," *Psychological Review*, 50:4 (1943), pp. 370–396.

11. C. S. Lewis, *The Four Loves* (London: G. Bles, 1960), pp. 10–30.

12. The myth is told in Aristophanes' speech in Plato's *Symposium* (189c-189d). trans. Christopher Gill (London: Penguin, 1999).

13. Noddings argues that caring is a kind of love that must be reciprocated. See her discussion in *Caring*, pp. 4–6.

14. Wagoner, *The Meanings of Love.*

15. Harry Frankfurt has a very interesting discussion on morality, favoring some more than others in *The Reasons of Love*, pp. 37–41. For Frankfurt, that we favor one over another makes common sense. This is also the case in traditional Confucian ethics. Though there is a strong sense that the virtuous person is one who demonstrates benevolence to all, there is a clear responsibility first to the immediate family. D. C. Lau comments, "following the footsteps of the Duke of Chou, Confucius made the natural love and obligations obtaining between members of the family the basis for general morality. . . . Love for people outside one's family is looked upon as an extension of the love for member's of one's own family. One consequence of this view is that the love, and so the obligation to love, decreases by degrees as it extends outwards. Geographically, one love's members of one's own family more than one's neighbours, one's neighbours more than one's fellow villagers, and so on." Introduction, to Confucius, *The Analects (Lun yü)*, trans. D. C. Lau (London: Penguin, 1979), p. 18.

16. Vladimir Solovyov says, "love is important not as one of our feelings, but as the transfer of all our interest in life from ourselves to another, as the shifting of the very center of our personal lives," *The Meaning of Love*, p. 51.

17. On romantic love see Irving Singer, *The Nature of Love 2*, and Mary Evans, *Love: An Unromantic Discussion* (Cambridge, Mass.: Polity, 2003). Singer looks historically at medieval courtly love, nineteenth-century romantic love, and the transition between the two. Evans analyzes and rejects the ideal of romantic love.

18. "Recognizing in love the truth of another, not abstractly, but essentially, transferring in deed the center of our life beyond the limits of our empirical personality, we by so doing reveal and realize our own real truth, our own absolute significance, which consists just in our capacity to transcend the borders of our factual phenomenal being, in our capacity to live not only in ourselves, but also in another," Solovyov, *The Meaning of Love*, p. 45.

19. Iris Murdoch, *The Black Prince* (Harmondsworth: Penguin, 1975).

20. Murdoch, *The Sea, the Sea* (London: Penguin Books, 1980).

21. For a creative argument that romantic love paves the way for *agapic* love, see Danielle Poe, "Romantic Love as an Entry to Agape," *The Acorn: Journal of the Gandhi-King Society*, 13:1 (2006), pp. 35–41.

22. See for example, among others, Julian of Norwich, *Revelations of Divine Love* (Short text and long Text), trans. Elizabeth Spearing (London: Penguin, 1998); Margery Kempe, *The Book of Margery Kempe*, trans. B. A. Windeatt (New York: Viking Penguin, 1985); Andy Fitz-Gibbon and Jane Fitz-Gibbon, *The Kiss of Intimacy: The Soul's Longing after God* (Crowborough: Monarch, 1985).

23. See for example, Solovyov says, "for good reason sexual relations are not merely termed love, but are also generally acknowledged to represent love *par excellence*, being the type and ideal of all other kinds of love (cf. *Song of Songs* and the *Apocalyse*)," *The Meaning of Love*, p. 42. Solovyov sees sexual love as the pinnacle of the evolutionary process, as humanity becomes more perfect, more divine, more in tune with universal consciousness—"the unity-of-the-all." (ibid.). p 40.

Act IV
Love's Appearance: Friendship, Affection, and Agape

1. Alfred North Whitehead: "The safest general characterization of the European philosophical tradition is that it consists of a series of footnotes to Plato," cited in Irving Singer, *The Nature of Love 1*, p. 47.

2. Plato, *Early Socratic Dialogues. (Ion, Laches, Lysis, Charmides, Hippias Major, Hippias Minor, Euthydemus)*, trans. Trevor J. Saunders, Iain lane, Donald Watt, and Robin Waterfield (London: Penguin, 1987).

3. Nora Ephron, *When Harry Met Sally*, dir. Rob Reiner, 1989.

4. Lewis said, "When two people who thus discover they are on the same secret road [of friendship] are of different sexes, the friendship which arise between them will very easily pass—may pass in the first half hour—into erotic love. Indeed, unless they are physically repulsive to each other, or unless one or both already loves elsewhere, it is almost certain to do so sooner or later," *The Four Loves*, p. 67.

5. Cicero, *De Senectute, De Amicitia, De Divinatione*, trans. William Armistead Falconer, Loeb Classical Library (Cambridge, Mass.: Harvard University Press, 1923).

6. Aelred, *Spiritual Friendship*, Cistercian Fathers Series, no. 5 (Washington, D.C.: Cistercian Publications Consortium Press, 1974). See also Brian Patrick McQuires, *Friendship and Community: The Monastic Experience 350–1250* (Kalamazoo, Mich.: Cistercian Publications, 1988).

7. Brian Patrick McQuire discusses Aelred and homosexuality in *Friendship and Community*, pp 302ff. He comments, "to ask whether Aelred actually 'had sex' with another man reflects perhaps our concerns more than Aelred's. For him what was important was not the act but the fire of desire that consumed him," p. 302. John Boswell comments, "there can be little question that Aelred was gay and that his erotic attraction to men was a dominant force in his life," *Christianity, Social Tolerance, and Homosexuality* (Chicago, Ill.: The University of Chicago Press, 1980), p. 222.

8. See discussion of Freud in Irving Singer, *The Nature of Love 3*, pp. 97–158.

9. Singer comments, "the suggestion that the psychoanalytic concept of sexuality coincides with Platonic eros seems wholly unwarranted. For Plato, eros was indeed a vital force that showed itself in the dynamism of sex. It explained the nature of sexual instinct, however, by revealing a search for perfection, a yearning for a highest good that did not exist in space or time and yet motivated the strivings of everything that did. Love (i.e., eros) being this 'desire for the perpetual possession of the Good,' Plato defines sexuality in terms of a yearning that is metaphysical, even spiritual," ibid., p. 99.

10. This is similar to the conclusion Alasdair MacIntyre draws at the end of *After Virtue*. "What matters at this stage is the construction of local forms of community within which civility and the intellectual and moral life can be sustained through the new dark ages which are already upon us," p. 262.

11. Gilligan, Carol, *In a Different Voice: Psychological Theory and Women's Development* (Cambridge: Harvard University Press, 1993).

12. The six stages were based on research during which Kohlberg followed eighty-four boys for twenty years. Women rarely reach beyond Kohlberg's third stage of moral development, where goodness is related in interpersonal terms and concerns helping and pleasing. For a discussion, see Gilligan, ibid., p. 18.

13. Noddings, *Caring*, p. 2.

14. Noddings says, "I shall reject the notion of universal love, finding it unattainable in any but the most abstract sense and thus a source of distraction," ibid. p. 29.

15. Virginia Held, in critiquing a paper by David Velleman, says, "he sees it as an attitude toward something universal—a rational nature of the status of being incomparable possessed by every person—in the beloved. The ethics of care, in contrast, would see the beloved herself as a unique, particular person to be valued for herself, rather than for her exemplification of something universal, and it would value the particular relation between the person and the beloved," in *The Ethics of Care: Personal, Political, and Global* (Oxford: Oxford University Press, 2006), p 91.

16. Peter Singer's utilitarian philosophy is exemplified in his 1999 piece for *New York Times Magazine*, "The Singer Solution to World Poverty," (5 September 1999), pp. 60–63. His view is that each person counts equally to every other person and that the moral obligation due to one is due to all.

17. Though Kwame Anthony Appiah acknowledges particularity in ethics, he affirms, "the idea that we have obligations to others, obligations that stretch beyond those to whom we are related by the ties of kith and kind, or even the formal ties of shared

citizenship," *Cosmopolitanism: Ethics in a World of Strangers* (New York: W.W. Norton, 2006), p. xv.

18. Martin Luther King Jr. evinced an eloquent understanding of agapic love: "*agape* means understanding, redeeming good will for all men. It is an overflowing love which is purely spontaneous, unmotivated, groundless, and creative. It is not set in motion by any quality or function of its object. It is the love of God operating in the human heart. *Agape* is disinterested love. It is love in which the individual seeks not his own good, but the good of his neighbor (1 Cor. 10:24). *Agape* does not begin by discriminating between worthy and unworthy people, or any qualities people possess. It begins by loving others *for their own sakes*. It is entirely 'neighbor-regarding concern for others,' which discovers the neighbor in every man it meets. Therefore, *agape* makes no distinction between friends and enemy; it is directed towards both." *A Testament of Hope: The Essential Writings of Martin Luther King, Jr.*, 1st ed. (San Francisco: Harper & Row, 1986), p. 19.

19. Sir John Templeton, *Agape Love: A Tradition Found in Eight World Religions* (Philadelphia , Penn.: Templeton Foundation Press, 1999). Templeton presents vignettes on love from Judaism, Christianity, Islam, Hinduism, Buddhism, Taoism, Confucianism, and Native Spirituality.

20. See, for example, Jane Goodall, "Helping Kin in Chimpanzees," in *Ethics*, ed. Peter Singer (Oxford: Oxford University Press, 1994), pp. 60–61.

21. In the *Grundlegung* (*Grounding for the Metaphysics of Morals*) (399), Kant says, "for love as an inclination cannot be commanded; but beneficence from duty, when no inclination impels us and even when a natural and unconquerable aversion opposes such beneficence, is practical, and not pathological, love. Such love resides in the will and not in the propensities of feeling, in principles of action and not in tender sympathy; and only the practical love can be commanded." See Ethical Philosophy, p. 12.

22. *Grundlegung* (429), ibid., p. 36.

Act V
Love Itself

1. Joseph Fletcher says, "the primary issue is the 'value' problem, and our choice of the summum bonum. This is the pre-ethical or metaethical question, relying on some other sources for a faith proposition or commitment. Only after this is settled can the method go to work, only after is knows what it is to seek or serve." *Situation Ethics*, p. 43.

2. Noddings argues that caring is the Good of human life. She says, "I am arguing that natural caring—some degree of which each of us has been dependent upon for our continued existence—is the natural state that we inevitably identify as 'good,'" *Caring*, p. 49.

3. MacIntyre, *After Virtue*, p. 148.

4. For a good explanation of the ontological argument, see Roy Jackson, *The God of Philosophy: An Introduction to the Philosophy of Religion* (London: The Philosopher's Magazine, 2001), pp. 52–66.

5. Though Anselm has had some supporters (notably Descartes) the strongest critique of Anselm came from Kant, who suggested that the fault with the argument was Anselm's use of "exist" as a predicate. Kant made a distinction between "logical"

and "real" predicates. A real predicate is one that determines, enlarges, or adds to our concept. He said that "God (subject) exists (predicate)" adds nothing to our concept of God, and so is a fallacy. See Jackson, ibid., pp. 60–61.

6. Hume has only a brief passage on the is/ought problem in Book III of *A Treatise on Human Nature* (London: Penguin, 1969). He says, "in every system of morality . . . the author proceeds for some time in the ordinary way of reasoning . . . when of a sudden I am surpriz'd to find, that instead of the usual copulations of propositions, is, and is not, I meet with no proposition that is not connected with an ought, or an ought not. . . . For an ought or an ought not, expresses some new relation or affirmation, 'tis necessary that it shou'd be observ'd and explain'd; and at the same time that a reason should be given, for what seems altogether inconceivable, how this new relation can be a deduction from others, which are entirely different from it," p. 521. For a good discussion of these issues, see W. D. Hudson, ed., *The Is/Ought Question* (Bristol: Macmillan, 1969).

7. This was the general approach of the logical positivists (the Vienna Circle during the early 1920s in Europe, and others, notably A. J. Ayer, outside their circle). In brief, the logical positivists argued for the "verification principle." Statements only have meaning if they can be verified empirically by sense experience (synthetic) or verified by the meaning of words and the grammar of the sentence structure (analytical). Ethical statements, aesthetics, and religious ideas could not be so verified and so were considered meaningless, neither true nor false. See A. J. Ayer, *Language, Truth and Logic* (New York: Dover, 1952). See also Hilary Putnam, *The Collapse of the Fact Value Dichotomy and Other Essays* (Cambridge: Harvard University Press, 2002).

8. See note 20 in Act I.

9. See note 24 in Act I. For a recent defense of ethical relativism, see Jesse J. Prinz, *The Emotional Construction of Morals* (Oxford: Oxford Univerity Press, 2007). Prinz argues that morality is based in emotion and that emotions, rather than being "hard-wired," are constructed by culture. As cultures differ, so do emotional responses, and therefore moral responses. Morality, then, is relative to the cultural construction of emotions.

10. See an extended argument against the fact/value dichotomy in Hilary Putnam, *The Collapse of the Fact/Value Dichotomy and Other Essays* (Cambridge: Harvard University press, 2002). Putnam argues that the idea that facts are objective and values subjective is a fantasy entertained by some philosophers of science.

11. Hume said, "reason is, and ought only to be the slave of the passions, and can never pretend to any other office than to serve and obey them" *A Treatise on Human Nature*, p. 462.

12. Plato has the soul as a charioteer driving two horses; one gentle that takes notice of the charioteer and the other crazed. *Pheadrus*, 246a-b, 253c-254e.

13. C. S. Lewis wrote an important little book in which he uses the Tao as a motif for those universal moral agreements of the great religious and philosophical traditions. See *The Abolition of Man; or, Reflections on Education with Special Reference to the Teaching of English in the Upper Forms of Schools* (New York: Macmillan, 1968).

14. Kierkegaard, *Works of Love.*
15. Kierkegaard, *Either/Or: A Fragment of Life*, ed. Victor Eremita, abridged and trans. Alastair Hanny (New York: Penguin, 1992).

Act VI
Love's Practice

1. MacIntyre says, "by a 'practice' I am going to mean any coherent and complex form of socially established cooperative human activity through which goods internal to that form of activity are realized in the course of trying to achieve those standards of excellence . . ." in *After Virtue*, p. 187.
2. See Emmanuel Levinas, *Otherwise than Being: Or Beyond Essence*, cited in Corey Beals, *Levinas and the Wisdom of Love* (Waco, Texas: Baylor University Press, 2007), p.162; and Luce Irigaray, *The Way of Love* (London, New York: Continuum, 2002), p.1.
3. See Andrew Fitz-Gibbon, "Is Love Nonviolent?" *The Acorn: Journal of the Gandhi-King Society*, 13:2 (Spring-Summer 2007), pp. 37–42.
4. See Andrew Fitz-Gibbon, "Rehabilitating Nonresistance," *The Acorn: Journal of the Gandhi-King Society*, 14:1 (Winter-Spring 2010), pp. 27–32.
5. See Gandhi, *Non-Violent Resistance (Satyagraha).*
6. See John Rawls, *A Theory of Justice* (Cambridge: Belknap Press, 1971).
7. His Holiness the Dalai Lama says, "I believe that if we stop to think, it is clear that our very survival, even today, depends upon the acts of kindness of so many people. Right from the moment of our birth, we are under the care and kindness of our parents; later in life, when facing the sufferings of disease and old age, we are again dependent on the kindness of others. If at the beginning and end of our lives we depend on others' kindness, why then in the middle, when we have opportunity, should we not act kindly toward others?" Foreword to Piero Ferrucci, *The Power of Kindness: The Unexpected Benefits of Leading a Compassionate Life* trans. Vivien Reid Ferrucci (New York: Jeremy P. Tarcher/Penguin, 2006), pp. ix–x.
8. Ibid. See also Lawrence G. Lovasik, *The Hidden Power of Kindness: A Practical Handbook for Souls Who Dare to Transform the World, One Deed at a Time* (Manchester, N.H.: Sophia Institute Press, 1962); and Adam Philips and Barbara Taylor, *On Kindness* (New York: Farrar, Straus, and Giroux, 2009). Phillips and Taylor look at kindness in much the way others look at compassion, sympathy, or love. They view kindness as rooted in biological instinct. Lovasik looks at kindness as a religious virtue; his work is full of references to theology and the Bible. Ferrucci looks at many aspects of kindness, which are not unlike my list of loves' virtues.
9. Ferrucci, *The Power of Kindness*, p. 7.
10. "this warre of every man against every man." Thomas Hobbes, *Leviathan* (London: Penguin 1968), p. 188.
11. For example, Virginia Held writes, "in this ethics, relationships between persons, rather than either individual rights or individual preferences, are a primary focus. Persons are seen as 'relational,' rather than as the self-sufficient individuals of traditional liberal theory. Caring relations are seen as being of central value." See *The Ethics of Care*, p. 119; and, "care ethics emerged as the gender bias of such dominant moral theories as Kantian ethics and utilitarianism came under attack . . . . In contrast the dominant views that gave primacy to such values as autonomy, in-

dependence, non-interference, fairness, and rights, the ethics of care values the in- terdependence and caring relations that connect persons to one another (p. 129). In *Maternal Thinking* (Boston: Beacon Press, 1989, 1995), Sara Ruddick deals extensively with peacemaking, justice, and feminist ethics.

12. In *About Love*, Robert Solomon says that [erosic] love is a process that takes time. Without faithfulness, the process that love is will never have opportunity to take place. He says, "love is an emotional process that not only takes time but also reaches into the future and builds its own foundation. It is not a momentary feel- ing or passion and it should not be conceived in the limited terms of initial attrac- tion and youthful first love, nor should it be overly domesticated or idealized. Love doesn't last because we misunderstand it, lose interest in it, take it for granted or suffocate it with careers and routines. Love last when it recognizes it- self as primary, when it faces up to its own difficulties, when it understands itself as a process rather than a passion," pp. 15–16.

13. For a very useful short summary of the value of attention, see Peck, *The Road Less Traveled*, pp. 120–131.

14. On mindfulness, see, for example, Jon Kabat-Zinn, *Coming to Our Senses: Healing the World through Mindfulness* (New York: Hyperion, 2005); and Thích Nhất Hạnh, *The Miracle of Mindfulness* (Boston: Beacon Press, 1975), *Peace Is Every Step: The Path of Mindfulness in Everyday Life* (New York: Bantam, 1991); and *Love in Action: Writings on Noviolent Social Change* (Berkeley, Ca- lif.: Parallax Press, 1993).

15. On non-attachment, see Peck, "Love as Separateness," in *The Road Less Traveled*, pp. 160–169.

BIBLIOGRAPHY

Aelred. *Spiritual Friendship*. Cistercian Fathers Series, no. 5. Washington, D.C.: Cistercian Publications Consortium Press, 1974.

American Psychiatric Association. *Diagnostic and Statistical Manual of Mental Disorders* (*DSM-IV*). Fourth Edition. Washington, D.C., 1994.

Amir, Lydia B. "Morality, Psychology, Philosophy," Philosophical Practice, 1:1 (2005), p. 53.

Anderson, Pamela Sue. *A Feminist Philosophy of Religion: The Rationality and Myths of Religious Belief.* Oxford and Malden: Blackwell, 1998.

Appiah, Kwame Anthony. *Cosmopolitanism: Ethics in a World of Strangers*. New York: W.W. Norton, 2006.

Arendt, Hannah. *The Life of the Mind*. Orlando, Fla.: Harcourt, 1978.

———, Joanna Vecchiarelli Scott, and Judith Chelius Stark. *Love and Saint Augustine*. Chicago, Ill.: The University of Chicago Press, 1996.

Augustine of Hippo. *City of God*. Translated by Henry Bettensen. London: Penguin, 2003.

Ayer, A. J. *Language, Truth and Logic*. New York: Dover, 1952.

Beals, Corey. *Levinas and the Wisdom of Love*. Waco, Tex.: Baylor University Press, 2007.

Bell, Daniel. *Communitarianism and Its Critics*. Oxford: Clarendon Press, 1993.

Bellah, Robert N. *Habits of the Heart: Individualism and Commitment in American Life*. Early: University of California Press, 1985.

Blackburn, Simon. *Being Good: A Short Introduction to Ethics*. Oxford: Oxford University Press, 2001.

———. *Ethics: A Very Short Introduction*. Oxford: Oxford University Press, 2001.

Boswell, John. *Christianity, Social Tolerance, and Homosexuality: Gay People in Western Europe from the Beginning of the Christian Era to the Fourteenth Century*. Chicago, Ill.: The University of Chicago Press, 1980.

Buber, Martin. *I and Thou*. Translated by Walter Kaufman. New York: Touchtone, 1970.

Buscaglia, Leo. *Love*. New York: Ballentine Books, 1982.

Cicero. *De Senectute, De Amicitia, De Divinatione*. Translated by William Armistead Falconer, Loeb Classical Library. Cambridge, Mass.: Harvard University Press, 1923.

Confucius. The Analects (Lun yü). Translated by D. C. Lau. London: Penguin, 1979.

Descartes, René. *Meditations on First Philosophy*. Indianapolis, Ind.: Bobbs-Merrill, 1960/1641.

Dickie, George. *Introduction to Aesthetics: An Analytical Approach*. Oxford: Oxford University Press, 1997.

Evans, Mary. *Love: An Unromantic Discussion*. Cambridge, Mass.: Polity, 2003.

Ferrucci, Piero. *The Power of Kindness: The Unexpected Benefits of Leading a Compassionate Life*. Translated by Vivien Reid Ferrucci. New York: Jeremy P. Tarcher/Penguin, 2006.

Fitz-Gibbon, Andrew. "Is Love Nonviolent?" *The Acorn: Journal of the Gandhi-King Society*, 13:2 (Spring-Summer 2007), pp. 37–42.

———. "Rehabilitating Nonresistance," *The Acorn: Journal of the Gandhi-King Society*, 14:1 (Winter-Spring 2010), pp. 27–32.

———. "Review of Eric Silverman, *The Prudence of Love: How Possessing the Virtue of Love Benefits the Lover*," *Teaching Philosophy* (March 2012).

Fitz-Gibbon, Andy, and Jane Fitz-Gibbon. *The Kiss of Intimacy: The Soul's Longing after God*. Crowborough: Monarch, 1995.

Fletcher, Joseph F. *Situation Ethics: The New Morality*. Philadelphia, Penn.: Westminster Press, 1966.

Frankfurt, Harry. *The Reasons of Love*. Princeton, N.J.: Princeton University Press, 2004.

Fromm, Erich. *The Art of Loving*. New York: Harper Perennials, 1956.

Gadamer, Hans Georg. *Truth and Method*. London: Sheed & Ward, 1975.

———, and David E. Linge. *Philosophical Hermeneutics*. Berkeley: University of California Press, 1976.

Gandhi, Mahatma. *Non-Violent Resistance (Satyagraha)*. Mineola, N.Y.: Dover, 2001.

———. *The Essential Gandhi, an Anthology*. Edited by Louis Fischer. New York: Random House, 2002.

———. *Gandhi's Experiments with Truth: Essential Writings by and about Mahatma Gandhi*. Edited by Richard L. Johnson. Lanham, Md.: Lexington Books, 2006.

Garrett, Brian. *What Is This Thing Called Metaphysics?* New York: Routledge, 2006.

Gilligan, Carol. *In a Different Voice: Psychological Theory and Women's Development*. Cambridge, Mass.: Harvard University Press, 1993.

Goodall, Jane. "Helping Kin in Chimpanzees." In *Ethics*. Edited by Peter Singer. Oxford: Oxford University Press, 1994.

Graves, Robert. *The Greek Myths*. London: Folio Society, 1996.

Griffin, James. *Value Judgment: Improving Our Ethical Beliefs*. Oxford: Clarendon Press, 1996.

Held, Virginia. *The Ethics of Care: Personal, Political, and Global*. Oxford: Oxford University Press, 2006.

Hobbes, Thomas. *Leviathan*. London: Penguin 1968.

Hudson, W. D., Ed. *The Is/Ought Question*. Bristol: Macmillan, 1969.

Hume, David. *A Treatise of Human Nature*. London: Penguin, 1969.

———. *An Enquiry Concerning the Principles of Morals*. Indianapolis: Hackett, 1983.

———. *David Hume: Moral Philosophy*. Edited by Geoffrey Sayre-McCord. Indianapolis, Ind.: Hackett, 2006.

Hutcheon, Pat Duffy. "Through a Glass Darkly: Freud's Concept of Love." In *The Nature and Pursuit of Love: The Philosophy of Irving Singer*, Edited by David Goicoechea. Amherst, N.Y.: Prometheus Books, 1995.

Huxley, Aldous. *The Perennial Philosophy*. New York: Harper Perennial, 2009.

Irigaray, Luce. *The Way of Love*. London, New York: Continuum, 2002.

Jackson, Roy. *The God of Philosophy: An Introduction to the Philosophy of Religion*. London: The Philosopher's Magazine, 2001.

Jantzen, Grace M. *Becoming Divine: Towards a Feminist Philosophy of Religion.* Bloomington and Indianapolis: Indiana University Press, 1999.

Julian of Norwich. *Revelations of Divine Love.* (Short text and long text) Translated by Elizabeth Spearing. London: Penguin, 1998.

Jung, C. G. *On the Nature of the Psyche.* New York: Modern Library: Random House, 1959.

Kabat-Zinn, Jon. *Coming to Our Senses: Healing the World through Mindfulness.* New York: Hyperion, 2005.

Kant, Immanuel. *Ethical Philosophy: The Complete Texts of Grounding for the Metaphysics of Morals and Metaphysical Principles of Virtue (Part II of the Metaphysics of Morals). [1785, 1797].* Translated by James W. Ellington. Indianapolis, Ind.: Hackett, 1983.

———. *Critique of Pure Reason.* Translated by J. M. D. Meiklejohn. Amherst, N.Y.: Prometheus Books, 1990.

———. *Critique of Practical Reason.* Translated by J. M. D. Meiklejohn. Amherst, N.Y.: Prometheus Books, 1990.

Kempe, Margery. *The Book of Margery Kempe.* Translated by B. A. Windeatt. New York: Viking Penguin, 1985.

Kierkegaard, Søren. *Works of Love: Kierkegaards's Writing.* Translated by Howard V. Hong and Edna H. Hong. Princeton, N.J. :Princeton University Press, 1962.

———. *Either/Or: A Fragment of Life.* Edited by Victor Eremita. Abridged and translated by Alastair Hanny. New York: Penguin, 1992.

King Jr., Martin Luther. *A Testament of Hope: The Essential Writings of Martin Luther King, Jr.* First Edition. San Francisco, Calif.: Harper & Row, 1986.

Laing, R. D. *The Divided Self.* London: Penguin, 1960.

Lewis, C. S. *The Four Loves.* London: G. Bles, 1960.

———. *The Abolition of Man; or, Reflections on Education with Special Reference to the Teaching of English in the Upper Forms of Schools.* New York: Macmillan, 1968.

Lewis, Thomas, Fari Amini, and Richard Lannon. *A General Theory of Love.* New York: Vintage Books, 2000.

Lovasik, Lawrence G. *The Hidden Power of Kindness: A Practical Handbook for Souls Who Dare to Transform the World, One Deed at a Time.* Manchester, N.H.: Sophia Institute Press, 1962.

MacIntyre, Alasdair. *A Short History of Ethics: A History of Moral Philosophy from the Homeric Age to the Twentieth Century.* London: Routledge, 1967.

———. *After Virtue: A Study in Moral Theory.* London: Gerald Duckworth, 1985.

———. *Whose Justice? Which Rationality?* London: Duckworth, 1988.

———. *Three Rival Versions of Moral Inquiry.* London: Duckworth, 1990.

Macmurray, John. *Reason and Emotion.* Second Edition. Amherst, N.Y.: Humanity Books, 1992.

Marx, Karl, and Friedrich Engels. *The Communist Manifesto.* Translated by Samuel Moore. London: Penguin, 1967.

Maslow, A. H. "A Theory of Human Motivation," *Psychological Review*, 50:4 (1943), pp. 370–396.

McQuires, Brian Patrick. *Friendship and Community: The Monastic Experience 350–1250.* Kalamazoo, Mich.: Cistercian Publications, 1988.

Midgley, Mary. *Can't We Make Moral Judgments?* New York: St. Martin's Press, 1993.

Moore, G. E. *Principia Ethica.* Amherst, N.Y.: Prometheus Books, 1988.

Murdoch, Iris. *The Black Prince.* Harmondsworth: Penguin, 1975.

———. *The Sovereignty of Good.* New York: Routledge, 1970.

———. *The Sea, the Sea.* London: Penguin Books, 1980.

———.*Metaphysics as a Guide to Morals.* New York: Allen Lane, Penguin, 1993.

Noddings, Nel. *Caring: A Feminine Approach to Ethics & Moral Education.* Berkeley: University of California Press, 2003.

———. *A Feminine Approach to Ethics & Moral Education.* Berkeley: University of California Press, 2003.

Nussbaum, Martha C. *Upheavals of Thought: The Intelligence of Emotions.* New York: Cambridge University Press, 2001.

O'Neil, Onora. "Kantian Ethics." *A Companion to Ethics.* Edited by Peter Singer. Cambridge: Blackwell, 1991.

Otto, Rudolf. *The Idea of the Holy: An Inquiry into the Non-Rational Factor in the Idea of the Divine and Its Relation to the Rational.* Translated by John W. Harvey. London: Oxford University Press, 1950.

Pascal, Blaise. *Pensées.* Edited and translated by Roger Ariew. Indianapolis, Ind.: Hackett, 2005.

Paul, Richard, and Linda Elder. *The Thinkers Guide to Fallacies.* Dillon Beach, Calif.: Foundation for Critical Thinking, 2004.

———. *The Miniature Guide to Understanding the Foundations of Ethical Reasoning.* Dillon Beach, Calif.: Foundation for Critical Thinking, 2005.

Peck, M. Scott. *The Road Less Traveled: A New Way of Love, Traditional Values and Spiritual Growth.* New York: Touchstone, 1978.

Philips, Adam,, and Barbara Taylor. *On Kindness.* New York: Farrar, Straus, and Giroux, 2009.

Plato. *Early Socratic Dialogues. (Ion, laches, Lysis, Charmides, Hippias Major, Hippias Minor, Euthydemus).* Translated by Trevor J. Saunders, Iain lane, Donald Watt, and Robin Waterfield. London: Penguin, 1987.

———. *The Republic.* Translated by Desmond Lee. London: Penguin, 1987.

———. *Symposium.* Translated by Christopher Gill. London: Penguin, 1999.

Pink, Thomas. *Free Will: A Very Short Introduction.* Oxford: Oxford University Press, 2004.

Poe, Danielle. "Romantic Love as an Entry to Agape," *The Acorn: Journal of the Gandhi-King Society,* 13:1 (2006), pp. 35–41.

Post, Stephen G. *Unlimited Love: Altruism, Compassion and Service.* Philadelphia, Penn.: Templeton Foundation Press, 2003.

Prinz, Jesse J. *The Emotional Construction of Morals.* Oxford: Oxford University Press, 2007.

Pritchard, Duncan. *What Is the Thing Called Knowledge?* New York: Routledge, 2006.

Putnam, Hilary. *The Collapse of the Fact Value Dichotomy and Other Essays.* Cambridge, Mass.: Harvard University Press, 2002.

Rachels, James, and Stuart Rachels. *The Elements of Moral Philosophy.* Sixth Edition. New York: McGraw Hill, 2010.

Rand, Ayn. *The Fountainhead.* London: Harper Collins, 1994.

————. *Atlas Shrugged.* London: Penguin, 2007.

Rawls, John. *A Theory of Justice.* Cambridge, Mass.: Belknap Press, 1971.

Roeser, Sabine. *Moral Emotions and Intuitions.* New York: Palgrave Macmillan, 2011.

Rogers, Carl. "Some Observations on the Organization of Personality," *American Psychologist*, 2 (1947), pp. 358–368.

Ross, David. *The Right and the Good.* Oxford: Oxford University Press, 2002.

Ruokonen, Floora. "Good, Self, and Un-selfing—Reflections on Iris Murdoch's Moral Philosophy," *Austrian Ludwig Wittgenstein Society* (2002), pp. 211–213.

Sartre, Jean-Paul. *Being and Nothingness: An Essay in Phenomenological Ontology.* Translated by Hazel Barnes. New York: Citadel Press, 2001.

Scruton, Roger. *Kant: A Very Short Introduction.* Oxford: Oxford University Press, 2001.

Silverman, Eric. *The Prudence of Love: How Possessing the Virtue of Love Benefits the Lover.* Lanham, Md.: Lexington Books, 2010.

Singer, Irving. *The Nature of Love 1: Plato to Luther.* Cambridge: The MIT Press, 2009.

————. *The Nature of Love 2: Courtly and Romantic.* Cambridge, Mass.: The MIT Press, 2009.

————. *The Nature of Love 3: The Modern World.* Cambridge, Mass.: The MIT Press, 2009.

————. *Philosophy of Love: A Partial Summing-Up.* Cambridge, Mass.: The MIT Press, 2009.

————. *The Pursuit of Love.* Baltimore, Md.: Johns Hopkins University Press, 1994.

Singer, Peter. "The Singer Solution to World Poverty," *New York Times Magazine* (5 September 1999), pp. 60–63.

Smith, Adam. *The Theory of Moral Sentiments.* Mineola, N.Y.: Dover Publications.

Soble, Alan. *Eros, Agape, and Philia: Readings in the Philosophy of Love.* New York: Paragon House Publishers, 1989.

————. *The Structure of Love.* New Haven, London: Yale University Press, 1990.

————. *The Philosophy of Sex and Love.* Second Edition. Edited by John K. Roth and Frederick Sontag. St. Paul, Minn.: Paragon House, 2008.

Solomon, Robert C. *The Passions: Emotions and the Meaning of Life.* Indianapolis, Ind.: Hackett, 1993.

————. *About Love: Reinventing Romance for Our Times.* Indianapolis, Ind.: Hackett, 1994.

————. *Not Passions Slave: Emotions and Choice.* Oxford: Oxford University Press, 2003.

————. *On Ethics and Living Well.* Belmont: Wadsworth/Thomson, 2006.

————, and Kathleen M. Higgins. *The Philosophy of (Erotic) Love.* Lawrence: University Press of Kansas, 1991.

Solovyov, Vladimir Sergeyevich. *The Meaning of Love*. Translated by Thomas R. Beyer. West Stockbridge, Mass.: Lindisfarne Press, 1985.

Sorokin, Pitirim A. *The Ways and Power of Love: Types, Factors, and Techniques of Moral Transformation*. Radnor, Penn.: Templeton Foundation Press, 1982.

Staub De Laszlo, Violet. *The Basic Writings of C. G. Jung*. New York: The Modern Library, 1993.

Templeton, Sir John. *Agape Love: A Tradition Found in Eight World Religions*. Philadelphia , Penn.: Templeton Foundation Press, 1999.

Thích Nhất Hạnh. *The Miracle of Mindfulness*. Boston, Mass.: Beacon Press, 1975.

————. *Peace Is Every Step: The Path of Mindfulness in Everyday Life*. New York: Bantam, 1991.

————. *Love in Action: Writings on Noviolent Social Change*. Berkeley, Calif.: Parallax Press, 1993.

Wagoner, Robert. *The Meanings of Love: An Introduction to Philosophy of Love*. Westport: Praeger, 1997.

Weber, Max. *The Sociology of Religion*. Boston, Mass.: Beacon Press, 1993.

ABOUT THE AUTHORS

ANDREW FITZ-GIBBON is Associate Professor of Philosophy, Chair of the Philosophy Department, and Director of the Center for Ethics, Peace, and Social Justice at the State University of New York College at Cortland. He earned his PhD from the University of Newcastle-upon-Tyne, UK. His academic interests are in the areas of ethics, nonviolence, love, mysticism, and community. He is the author, co-author, or editor of seven books, numerous book chapters, and articles in peer reviewed journals such as *Social Philosophy Today, The Journal for Peace and Justice Studies, The Acorn,* and *Philosophical Practice.* He is an Associate Editor, VIBS, Editions Rodopi, B.V., where he edits the Social Philosophy Series. He is a fellow of the American Philosophical Practitioners Association, certified in client counseling, and is abbot of the Lindisfarne Community, a small ecumenical religious order in Ithaca, New York.

BARRY L. GAN is Professor of Philosophy and Director of the Center for Nonviolence at St. Bonaventure University. He is co-editor with Robert L. Holmes of a leading anthology on nonviolence, *Nonviolence in Theory and Practice* (second edition, 2005, now in its third edition); editor of *The Acorn: Journal of the Gandhi-King Society*; former co-editor of *Peace and Change: A Journal of Peace Research* and *Journal of the Peace History Society and the Peace and Justice Studies Association.* For two years, he served as program committee chair of the Fellowship of Reconciliation, the oldest and largest interfaith peace group in the United States. Gan has taught at St. Bonaventure University for the past twenty-eight years, since receiving his MA (1981) and PhD (1984) in philosophy from the University of Rochester. Prior to his appointment at St. Bonaventure, he taught high school and junior high school English for six years.

INDEX

sex, *con't.*
   love vs. s., 47
   s. relations vs. love, 120n23
shoulds, 22
Singer, Irving, 4, 64
situationism, 11
Smith, Adam, 19
Soble, Alan, 4
social:
   meaning of "s." in philosophy, 22
   s. revolutions, 3
   s. roles, 38
Sociology of Religion (Weber), 34
sociopathy, 10
solitude, 22
Solomon, Robert, 9
Stoicism, 14
subject/object criterion, 20
suffering, 72, 76, 77
suicide, 23, 24
sympathy, 5, 9, 12, 19, 84–86
   innate s., 10

tel(eology)(os) , 33, 68, 74, 89, 92, 93,
   118n3
   chosen vs. God-given t., 69
   elective t., 32, 91
   love chosen as t. of humanity, 72
Templeton, Sir John, 65
tenderness, 99, 100

thankfulness, 93, 106
theology, Augustinian t., 32
thriving. *See* flourishing
transformation through love, 49, 50
trust, 103, 105
truth(fulness), 81, 89, 112n16
   potential for pain in knowing t., 70

universal(ism)(s), 6, 43
"us" and "we," exlusionary use of, 36
utilitarianism, 11, 28, 70

verifiability and meaning, 123n7
verification principle, 123n7
violence, 79
   greater good, v. demanded for, 96
virtue(s), 26–28, 32, 33, 92, 97–99, 104,
   107, 108
   feminine (softer), 101
   feminine v., 100
   state and action, v. as both, 94
Wagoner, Robert, 40
Weber, Max, 34
well-being, 71, 72, 89, 116n9
When Harry Met Sally, 55
wisdom, 93, 94
   Jewish w., 5
   love-itself and w., 93
Zen tradition, 106

VIBS

The **Value Inquiry Book Series** is co-sponsored by:

Titles Published

Volumes 1 - 213 see www.rodopi.nl

214. Matti Häyry, Tuija Takala, Peter Herissone-Kelly and Gardar Árnason, Editors, *Arguments and Analysis in Bioethics*. A volume in **Values in Bioethics**

215. Anders Nordgren, *For Our Children: The Ethics of Animal Experimentation in the Age of Genetic Engineering*. A volume in **Values in Bioethics**

216. James R. Watson, Editor, *Metacide: In the Pursuit of Excellence*. A volume in **Holocaust and Genocide Studies**

217. Andrew Fitz-Gibbon, Editor, *Positive Peace: Reflections on Peace Education, Nonviolence, and Social Change*. A volume in **Philosophy of Peace**

218. Christopher Berry Gray, *The Methodology of Maurice Hauriou: Legal, Sociological, Philosophical*. A volume in **Studies in Jurisprudence**

219. Mary K. Bloodsworth-Lugo and Carmen R. Lugo-Lugo, *Containing (Un)American Bodies: Race, Sexuality, and Post-9/11 Constructions of Citizenship*. A volume in **Philosophy of Peace**

220. Roland Faber, Brian G. Henning, Clinton Combs, Editors, *Beyond Metaphysics? Explorations in Alfred North Whitehead's Late Thought*. A volume in **Contemporary Whitehead Studies**

221. John G. McGraw, *Intimacy and Isolation (Intimacy and Aloneness: A Multi-Volume Study in Philosophical Psychology, Volume One)*, A volume in **Philosophy and Psychology**

222. Janice L. Schultz-Aldrich, Introduction and Edition, *"Truth" is a Divine Name, Hitherto Unpublished Papers of Edward A. Synan, 1918-1997*. A volume in **Gilson Studies**

223. Larry A. Hickman, Matthew Caleb Flamm, Krzysztof Piotr Skowroński and Jennifer A. Rea, Editors, *The Continuing Relevance of John Dewey: Reflections on Aesthetics, Morality, Science, and Society*. A volume in **Central European Value Studies**

224. Hugh P. McDonald, *Creative Actualization: A Meliorist Theory of Values*. A volume in **Studies in Pragmatism and Values**

225. Rob Gildert and Dennis Rothermel, Editors, *Remembrance and Reconciliation*. A volume in **Philosophy of Peace**

226. Leonidas Donskis, Editor, *Niccolò Machiavelli: History, Power, and Virtue*. A volume in **Philosophy, Literature, and Politics**

227. Sanya Osha, *Postethnophilosophy*. A volume in **Social Philosophy**

228. Rosa M. Calcaterra, Editor, *New Perspectives on Pragmatism and Analytic Philosophy*. A volume in **Studies in Pragmatism and Values**

229. Danielle Poe, Editor, *Communities of Peace: Confronting Injustice and Creating Justice*. A volume in **Philosophy of Peace**

230. Thorsten Botz-Bornstein, Editor, *The Philosophy of Viagra: Bioethical Responses to the Viagrification of the Modern World*. A volume in **Philosophy of Sex and Love**

231. Carolyn Swanson, *Reburial of Nonexistents: Reconsidering the Meinong-Russell Debate*. A volume in **Central European Value Studies**

232. Adrianne Leigh McEvoy, Editor, *Sex, Love, and Friendship: Studies of the Society for the Philosophy of Sex and Love: 1993–2003*. A volume in **Histories and Addresses of Philosophical Societies**

233. Amihud Gilead, *The Privacy of the Psychical*. A volume in **Philosophy and Psychology**

234. Paul Kriese and Randall E. Osborne, Editors, *Social Justice, Poverty and Race: Normative and Empirical Points of View*. A volume in **Studies in Jurisprudence**

235. Hakam H. Al-Shawi, *Reconstructing Subjects: A Philosophical Critique of Psychotherapy*. A volume in **Philosophy and Psychology**

236. Maurice Hauriou, *Tradition in Social Science*. Translation from French with an Introduction by Christopher Berry Gray. A volume in **Studies in Jurisprudence**

237. Camila Loew, *The Memory of Pain: Women's Testimonies of the Holocaust.*. A volume in **Holocaust and Genocide Studies**

238. Stefano Franchi and Francesco Bianchini, Editors, *The Search for a Theory of Cognition: Early Mechanisms and New Ideas.* A volume in **Cognitive Science**

239. Michael H. Mitias, *Friendship: A Central Moral Value.* A volume in **Ethical Theory and Practice**

240. John Ryder and Radim Šíp, Editors, *Identity and Social Transformation, Central European Pragmatist Forum, Volume Five.* A volume in **Central European Value Studies**

241. William Sweet and Hendrik Hart, *Responses to the Enlightenment: An Exchange on Foundations, Faith, and Community.* A volume in **Philosophy and Religion**

242. Leonidas Donskis and J.D. Mininger, Editors, *Politics Otherwise: Shakespeare as Social and Political Critique.* A volume in **Philosophy, Literature, and Politics**

243. Hugh P. McDonald, *Speculative Evaluations: Essays on a Pluralistic Universe.* A volume in **Studies in Pragmatism and Values.**

244. Dorota Koczanowicz and Wojciech Małecki, Editors, *Shusterman's Pragmatism: Between Literature and Somaesthetics.* A volume in **Central European Value Studies**

245. Harry Lesser, Editor, *Justice for Older People,* A volume in **Values in Bioethics**

246. John G. McGraw, *Personality Disorders and States of Aloneness (Intimacy and Aloneness: A Multi-Volume Study in Philosophical Psychology, Volume Two),* A volume in **Philosophy and Psychology**

247. André Mineau, *SS Thinking and the Holocaust.* A volume in **Holocaust and Genocide Studies**

248. Yuval Lurie, *Wittgenstein on the Human Spirit.* A volume in **Philosophy, Literature, and Politics**

249. Andrew Fitz-Gibbon, *Love as a Guide to Morals.* A volume in **Ethical Theory and Practice**

Lightning Source UK Ltd.
Milton Keynes UK
UKOW052025060812

197135UK00002B/126/P